Basic Christian Beliefs

Holman Reference

Nashville, Tennessee

ISBN: 978-0-8054-9500-3

Design copyright ©2005 LionHudson plc/
Tim Dowley and Peter Wyart trading as Three's
Company

Dewey Decimal Classification: 230.0
Subject Heading: Theology, Doctrinal

Worldwide co-edition produced by
Lion Hudson plc
Wilkinson House,
Jordan Hill Road,
Oxford OX2 8DR,
England
Tel: +44 (0) 1865 302750
Fax:+44 (0) 1854 303757
e-mail:coed@lionhudson.com
www.lionhudson.com

1 2 3 4 5 6   11 10 09 08 07
LH

Printed in Singapore

Contents

How to Use This book

DESIGNED FOR THE BUSY USER

Illustrated Bible Summary Series is designed to provide an easy-to-use tool that incorporates information from a variety of sources. This brings you the benefits of many more advanced and expensive works packed into one small volume.

This series is for laymen, pastors, teachers, small-group leaders and participants, as well as the classroom student. Enrich your personal study or quiet time. Shorten your class or small-group preparation time as you gain valuable insights in the truths of God's Word that you can pass along to your students or group members.

DESIGNED FOR QUICK ACCESS

Those with time constraints will especially appreciate the timesaving features built in the *Illustrated Bible Summary Series*.

CONCISE INFORMATION. *Basic Christian Beliefs* summarizes a vast amount of information.

ICONS. Various icons in the margin highlight points of interest that enhance the study of Christian theology.

SIDEBARS AND CHARTS. These specially selected features make it easier to grasp key points.

DESIGNED TO WORK FOR YOU

PERSONAL STUDY. At your fingertips is information that would require searching several volumes to find.

TEACHING. *The Illustrated Bible Summary Series* is helpful to teachers. Its compact format facilitates gaining a quick overview of the major themes of Christian theology and structuring those themes in a teaching context.

GROUP STUDY. *The Illustrated Bible Summary Series* in the hands of individual participants will enrich group studies of studies on Christian theology.

LIST OF MARGIN ICONS USED IN
BASIC CHRISTIAN BELIEFS

Historical Context
Indicates background information—historical, biographical, cultural—that illuminates Christian doctrine.

Old Testament
Passages that enrich the reader's understanding of the Old Testament foundation of Christian belief.

New Testament
Scriptures from both the Gospels, Epistles, and Revelation that have shaped Christian theology.

Word Picture
Explanations of terms or expressions that elucidate Christian belief.

Quotes
Quotations from Christians across two millennia that amplify Christianity's core teachings.

Christian Theology

An Overview

Peanuts characters Lucy and Linus are both staring out the window as the rain is pouring down.

Lucy: *"Boy, look at it rain. What if it floods the whole world?"*

Linus: *"It will never do that. In the ninth chapter of Genesis, God promised Noah that would never happen again, and the sign of the promise is the rainbow."*

Lucy looks directly at Linus, turns back toward the window, smiles big and announces:

"You have taken a great load off of my mind."

To which Linus responds: *"Sound theology has a way of doing that!"*

These are wise and timely words from Linus. With feelings of fear and uncertainty abounding while we watch events from our windows, many of us hear least what we need most. Ignorance is not bliss when it comes to thinking about God.

We don't want those who design the aircraft we fly in to be ignorant of the laws of aerodynamics. We want their beliefs about aerodynamics to be as sound as possible.

We want our surgeons to have sound beliefs regarding how the human body functions.

If we are so concerned about the beliefs of aeronautical engineers and surgeons, how much more should all of us be concerned about the soundness of our beliefs about God.

Engineers' and surgeons' beliefs have significant consequences in this life. Our beliefs about God have significant consequences for now and for all eternity.

Theology—the beliefs we have about God—is the foundation for all of life. Everybody—atheists included—has a theology they live by. Theology is either sound or it is unsound. One of the most impor-

"Ezra had determined in his heart to study the law of the LORD, obey [it], and teach [its] statutes and ordinances in Israel (Ezra 7:10).

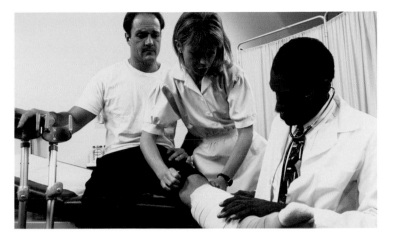

tant tasks of every human being is to discover and live by beliefs about the ultimate nature of reality that are true.

Jesus challenged His followers to teach others what they had learned from Him and had been commanded by Him (Matt. 28:18–20). Similarly, the New Testament epistles stress the importance of teaching and living "in accord with sound doctrine" (Titus 2:1, NIV). Christian truth must be formulated and articulated in such a way as to inform and shape beliefs, values, and lifestyles. The earliest form of Christian theology focused on Jesus and the teachings of the apostles. It was the responsibility of the first generation to encourage others by sound doctrine and refute those who opposed it (Titus 1:9).

Surgeon's beliefs have significant consequences in this life; our beliefs about God have significant consequences for all eternity.

What Is Christian Theology?

Christian theology forms the foundation of the church's beliefs, proclamation, and ministry. It not only involves believing revealed truth, but it also includes calling the church to purity and ethical holiness. Christian theology is the study of God and His works. It is not an exercise done in the ivory tower by specialists. No, theology is the responsibility of the church seeking to communicate what the church believes, primarily for believers, but also for others. Someone has said that theology is thinking about God. If that is the case, then everyone who seriously contemplates the greatness of the Creator God is in some sense a theologian.

The word *theology* comes from two Greek terms: *theos,* meaning

"Be diligent to present yourself approved to God, a worker who doesn't need to be ashamed, correctly teaching the word of truth" (2 Tim. 2:15).

The word theology is derived from two Greek words, *theos,* "God," and *logos,* "reason, order, word," and the like. In modern English usage such etymology is normally taken to mean that "theology" is the ordered consideration or study of God.

"God," and *logos,* meaning "word, expression, study of." Our task then is to think rightly about God based on what He has revealed about Himself in His Word, the Bible. Ultimately it may not matter what we think about baseball, movies, or politics, but it does matter what we think about God.

Jesus said that the greatest commandment is to love God with our heart, soul, mind, and strength. The purpose of theology is to help believers love God through an understanding of His person, work, and Word and to produce a love for neighbor and an understanding of self (see Matt. 22:37–39).

Is Theology Divisive or Distracting?

Some think theology is divisive so we should de-emphasize its importance. But theology is the backbone of the church. Without good theology the church cannot and will not mature in the faith. The apostle Paul says that believers with an immature faith will be "tossed back and forth by the waves, and blown here and there by every wind of teaching" (Eph. 4:14, NIV).

Healthy theology that matures the heart and head not only ena-

Martin Luther. Without good theology the Church will not mature in faith.

bles believers to move toward maturity, but it results in the worship and exaltation of God. Good theology leads to doxology. After eleven chapters of Paul's expounding the doctrine of sin, justification, sanctification, and the future of Israel, the apostle concludes by writing:

> Oh, the depth of the riches both of the wisdom and the
>   knowledge of God!
> How unsearchable His judgments and untraceable His ways!
> For who has known the mind of the Lord?
> Or who has been His counselor?
> Or who has ever first given to Him, and has to be repaid?
> For from Him and through Him and to Him are all things.
> To Him be the glory forever. Amen.
>   —Romans 11:33–36

While it may be true that the writings of some theologians unduly complicate the Christian faith or distract us from aspects of the Christian life like evangelism and worship, we should not conclude that theology itself is distracting or divisive. Evangelism based on unsound theology will be unsound and even dangerous. Worship that does not see God as He has revealed Himself does not rightly glorify God. Theology can help us better understand the faith we desire to share in our evangelistic efforts and, moreover, can help lead us to an awareness of the grandeur, greatness, and goodness of God, whom we worship.

66

"Evangelical theology aims not only to be faithful to Scripture, but also to explore the unfaithfulness of the Christian community to Scripture"—Donald G. Bloesch, *Essentials of Evangelical Theology* (San Francisco: Harper, 1978), 1:18.

99

What Is the Source and Goal of Theology?

Our primary source of theology is Holy Scripture. Though we learn much from God's revelation in nature and our own experience, these matters must be tested by God's Word in Scripture. It is important for us to recognize what others have thought about these matters, for in many ways we stand on their shoulders as we seek to communicate the meaning of the Christian faith that was once for all entrusted to the saints (Jude 3).

Our goal in this book is to outline the key themes of theology in a way that will exalt God and encourage believers in their Christian living. We will seek to address the important issues of our day, grounded in Holy Scripture, and stated in a contemporary and understandable way. Theology equips and encourages believers in their relationship with God.

Why Do We Need Theology?

Everyone has a theology. Everyone has beliefs about the ultimate nature of reality and those beliefs govern one's thinking, attitudes, and actions. If everyone has a different theology, not all of these theologies are true. These various theologies contradict one another, and contradictory beliefs can't both be true.

How do we know that our theology is true and sound? This is an important question because of the large number of challenges to the church at this time, including unbelief, cults, the rise of the new age, secular and postmodern worldviews.

We can do theology with confidence because God has revealed Himself in a meaningful way to His people (1 Cor. 2:10). Humans have been created in the image of God. As rational beings, we can think God's thoughts after Him and organize these thoughts. Believers can know and experience God because our hearts and minds have been made new by God's regenerating grace and thus we can interpret and apply Holy Scripture. This ability to perceive spiritual truth is made possible by the illuminating work of the Holy Spirit (1 Cor. 2:14–15; Ps. 119:18). It follows then that only Spirit-enabled Christians can do theology in a way that is pleasing to God.

The cross is at the center of Christian theology.

66

Theology enables God's people to recover a true understanding of human life, a sense of the greatness of the soul. It helps us recover the awareness that God is more important than we are, that the future life is more important than this one. A right view of God gives genuine significance and security to our lives. We understand that happiness is the promise of heaven and that holiness is the priority here in this world.

"Evangelical Christianity is theological in its character, biblical in its substance . . . and fundamental in its emphasis"—John R. W. Stott, *Christ the Controversialist* (London: Tyndale, 1970)

99

We can better understand what we believe and why we believe it. We can appreciate our heritage and enliven our future hope. The truth content of the faith can be preserved. It is the express task of theology to expound the whole counsel of God (Acts 20:7).

The church can be strengthened. The gospel, in its fullness, can be proclaimed. Without the foundation of solid theology, there can be no effective long-term preaching, evangelism, or missionary outreach. Those who would suggest that "what you don't know can't hurt you" could find themselves in great difficulty if this approach is taken toward ultimate matters like heaven and hell. On the other hand, sound, reliable theology, based squarely on God's Word, offers reassurance and hope. As we begin this study, we do so with a commitment to Scripture as the primary source of our theology. We need to hear what God has said and rest our case there. The sections that follow summarize the basic truths of the Christian faith concerning God, His Word, His World, Jesus Christ, the Holy Spirit, salvation, the Christian life, the church, and the rule and reign of God.

Further Reflection

1. What are the practical benefits of studying theology?
2. How will the study of theology impact our worship of God?

Foundation for Christian Theology

The Canon

Canon is a Latin word that means "ruler, rule, standard, or model." At the Bureau of Standards, there is a standard inch, against which all other inches are measured. Canonization is the process whereby certain books became part of the library we call Holy Scripture. This library of books is the standard against which beliefs and opinions are tested.

What is the Bible? Why is it important? These are most important questions about the book that has by far been the bestseller of all history and has been translated into more languages than any other book.

For years Christians have discussed and debated the nature of biblical authority. Strident controversies present in both church and society in many ways demonstrate the crisis of biblical authority. The hot item agenda questions facing the church such as abortion, homosexuality, postmodern concerns, and new age mysticism point to the wide-ranging gap between the message of Holy Scripture and beliefs that are widely held in our society. Our view of Scripture and its authority will largely determine where we stand on these hot issues. It is vitally important that Christians understand what is at stake in how they view the Bible and how they relate to the Bible day-to-day.

The Bible describes itself as a special book. Even before the canonization of the sacred books, importance was attached to the sacred writings. Moses wrote "everything the Lord had said" in the "Book of the Covenant" (Exod. 24:4, 7, NIV). Joshua's farewell address was written "in the Book of the Law of God" (Josh. 24:26). Samuel spoke words about the manner of the kingdom and "wrote them down on a scroll and deposited it before the Lord" (1 Sam. 10:25). Jesus repeatedly appealed to the authoritative Scriptures (see Matt. 19:4; 22:29). Similarly, Paul and the apostles thought of the scrolls as the "very words of God" (Rom. 3:2).

Jesus Himself declared that Scripture is the Word of God that cannot be broken (see John 10:35). It is "the word of the prophets made more certain" about which the apostles wrote, because these words were spoken from God as the writers "were carried along by the

Moses with the Ten Commandments

Holy Spirit" (2 Pet. 1:19–21). The Bible itself acknowledges that the prophetic-apostolic word is God's Word written. Without this writing there would be no Scriptures and therefore no Word of God available to us.

God's Revelation

The Bible affirms that God has made Himself known in a variety of ways (Ps. 19:1; Heb. 1:2). God has not abandoned us but has manifested Himself to us. We know Him not as a result of our seeking Him. God has acted and spoken in history.

The word *revelation* means "an uncovering, a removal of the veil, a disclosure of what was previously not known." More specifically, revelation is God's manifestation of Himself to humankind in such a way that men and women can know and have fellowship with Him.

Revelation is often discussed in two different categories: general and special. General revelation is universal in the sense that it is God's self-disclosure of Himself in a general way to all people at all times in all places. General revelation occurs through nature, through human experiences and conscience, and through his-

St Catherine's Monastery, Sinai

"Your word is a lamp to my feet and a light on my path"
(Ps. 119:105).

tory. God's general revelation is plain, though often misinterpreted because sinful and finite humans are trying to understand a perfect and infinite God. General revelation discloses God clearly enough to sinful human beings that they are responsible for their responses. Therefore, no one can be excused for missing God's revelation (Rom. 1:20; 3:20).

The light of nature, including conscience, is not sufficient to import the knowledge of God necessary for salvation. What is needed to understand God's self-disclosure fully is His special revelation. Indeed, special revelation provides the viewpoint through which we can fully understand and appreciate God's general revelation. Divine truth exists outside special revelation, but it is consistent with and supplemental to, not a substitute for, special revelation. General revelation is consistent with special revelation yet distinct from it. In contrast to God's general revelation, which is available to all people, God's special revelation is available to specific people at specific times in specific places.

Special revelation is not only particular, but progressive; not only propositional, but personal. The content of special revelation is primarily God Himself, His works and His word. It is the declaration of truth about God, His character, and His actions and relationship with His creation. God is pleased to reveal Himself and His majestic Word to people of faith. Our response of faith to God's Word, recorded and

Mount Sinai

interpreted by the prophets and the apostles, calls for us to embrace with humility and teachable hearts, without finding fault, whatever is taught in Holy Scripture.

The Bible's Message

The Bible presents a message about God and His purposes. It describes the creation of the universe, including the direct creation of men and women in a paradise on earth. The Bible describes the call of Abraham, the giving of the Law, the establishment of the kingdom, the division of the kingdom, and the captivity and restoration of Israel. Scripture sees humankind as fallen from a sinless condition and separated from God. The promise of a coming Messiah who will redeem men and women and reign as King appears throughout the Old Testament. The message of the Word of God claims that believers are restored to favor with God through the sacrifice of Christ.

The confession of Jesus as the Christ, the Savior of the world, is at the heart of the Christian faith. This message is central to the content of Holy Scriptures. Contemporary Christians need not only to affirm this message but also to affirm the Bible's inspiration, truthfulness, and normative nature. In the midst of the crisis of biblical authority in which we find ourselves, we need to evidence our concern for biblical authority by careful theological reflection, faithful proclamation, repentance, and prayer. A confession that the Bible is fully inspired and totally truthful is important because it is the foundation that establishes the complete extent of the Scripture's authority.

Contemporary Christians must choose to articulate a view of the Bible for the contemporary community that is faithful to and in continuity with the consensus of historic positions in the church that have characteristically confessed that the Bible is the written Word of God. Building upon that foundation block, we can relate to one another in love and humility, bringing about truth, fellowship, and community and resulting not only in right doctrine, but also in right practice before a watching world.

The Bible's Inspiration

Through the superintending influence of God's Spirit upon the writers of Holy Scripture, the account and interpretation of God's revelation has been recorded as God intended so that the Bible is actually the Word of God. In writing, these men of God used their

Part of the Old Testament inscribed on a fragment from a Dead Sea Scroll

own ordinary languages and literary forms that were typical of their day. Yet within this very human activity, God was at work. God chose to convey His Word through their words.

God's inspired Word came to us through human authors. It is actually possible to see different personalities as we look at various books of the Bible. The style, vocabulary, and particular purposes of the apostle John, for example, are distinct from those of Luke. Yet both final products of their writings are equally the inspired Word of God.

In the history of the church, the divine character of Scripture has been the great presupposition for the whole of Christian preaching

"The authority of the Holy Scripture, for which it ought to be believed and obeyed, dependeth not upon the testimony of any man or church, but wholly upon God (who is truth), the Author thereof; and therefore it is to be received, because it is the Word of God"
—I:4, Westminster Confession, 1646.

and theology. This is readily apparent in the way the New Testament speaks about the Old Testament. That which appears in the Old Testament is cited in the New Testament with formulas like "God said" and "The Holy Spirit says" (Acts 4:24–25; 13:47; 2 Cor. 6:16). Scripture and God are so closely joined together in the minds of New Testament authors that they naturally could speak of Scripture doing what it records God as doing (Gal. 3:8; Rom. 9:17). The introductory phrase "it stands written" is used as a stamp of authority on both Old and New Testament writings.

Because of the apostolic word's divine origin and content, Scripture can be described as certain and trustworthy (2 Pet. 1:19; cf. 1 Pet. 1:24–25). As a result, those who build their lives on Scripture "will never be put to shame" (1 Pet. 2:6). The Word was written for instruction and encouragement (Rom. 15:4), to lead to saving faith (2 Tim. 3:15), to guide people toward godliness (2 Tim. 3:16b), and to equip believers for good works (2 Tim. 3:17).

Second Timothy 3:16–17 focuses primarily on the product of inspiration, the final writing of Scripture, though it also includes secondary aspects of the purpose and process. What is being asserted is the activity of God throughout the entire process, so that the completed, final product ultimately comes from Him. It is a mistake to think of inspiration only in terms of the time when the Spirit moved the human author to write. The biblical concept of inspiration allows for the activity of the Spirit in special ways in the process without requiring that we understand all of the Spirit's working in one and the same way. In the process of creation and preservation of the universe, God providentially intervened in special ways for special purposes. Alongside and within this superintending action of the Spirit to inspire human writings in the biblical books, we likewise can affirm a special work of the Spirit in bringing God's revelation to the apostles and prophets. God's Spirit is involved both in revealing specific messages to the prophets (Jer. 1:1–9) and in guiding the authors of the historical section in their research (Luke 1:1–4).

We can assert that inspiration extends to the choice of words, even though Scripture's meaning is located at the sentence level and beyond. Thus our understanding of inspiration affirms the dual nature of Holy Scripture; it is a divine-human book. This recognition enables us to have a healthy understanding of the diverse literary genres represented in Scripture. The Holy Spirit is the one who, in a

The Bible affirms its own inspiration in 2 Timothy 3:16–17: "All Scripture is inspired by God and is profitable for teaching, for rebuking, for correcting, for training in righteousness, so that the man of God may be complete, equipped for every good work".

"

"Biblical inspiration is that supernatural influence of the Holy Spirit upon the Scripture writers which rendered their writings an accurate record of the revelation or which resulted in what they wrote actually being the Word of God"—Millard J. Erickson, *Christian Theology* (Grand Rapids: Baker, 1983–85), 199.

"

The New Testament books were written on scrolls.

mystery for which the Incarnation of Jesus Christ provides the only analogy, causes the verbal human witness to coincide with God's witness to Himself. Sometimes we think of God's action and human action as mutually exclusive. If God did something, humans didn't do it. But that's not the case. Some actions can be fully human and fully divine.

The Bible's Truthfulness and Authority

The result of our affirmations about a full view of inspiration calls for a commitment to the Bible's full truthfulness and sole authority. We believe the idea of a completely true Bible is important and adequately describes the results of inspiration. To affirm that the Bible is completely true means that it is trustworthy, reliable, infallible, and inerrant. To affirm the Bible's inerrancy means that "when all the facts are known, the Bible (in its autographs) properly interpreted in light of which culture and communication means had developed by the time of its composition, will be shown to be completely true (and therefore not false) in all that it affirms, to the degree of precision intended by the author, in all matters relating to God and His creation."

Genre is a type of literary composition. The Bible contains a rich variety of genres: history, narrative, poetry, law, prophecy, proverbs, Gospels, letters, and apocalyptic literature.

This definition of the Bible's complete truthfulness recognizes our need to approach Scripture in humble submission in awareness of God's omniscience and our own finitude. Instead of maintaining the critic's relative omniscience, we think it best to admit our own fallibility as critics and trust the omnipotent and omniscient work of God over and through the biblical writers.

While some continue to question the importance of an affirmation of the Bible's truthfulness or inerrancy, this confession is important for the church not because inerrancy is necessary for salvation but because it represents the Bible's own account of itself.

An affirmation that the Bible is inerrant or completely truthful is the necessary corollary of inspiration and primarily stresses the trustworthy character of God's faithful revelation to humanity. This confession recognizes that the Bible must be interpreted, but most importantly it interprets us.

An affirmation of the Bible's truthfulness does not imply an exhaustive knowledge of God or any other subject. Neither does it deny human authorship, promise a correct interpretation of Scripture, nor guarantee an accurate preservation of Scripture so as to produce inerrant translations. It does, however, set certain limits upon the range of acceptable answers in the matters of biblical interpretation and ultimately provides a solid foundation for trustworthy translations of Scripture.

As many orthodox theologians have observed, theology that does not confess the Bible's complete truthfulness and authority operates within the circle of human concepts and experience and has no reference point. A renewed commitment to the Bible's full inspiration, truthfulness, and authority is the first step toward healing the deadly sickness in today's theological trends. Believing the Bible to be inspired and true, we can joyfully and confidently commit our lives to its message and gladly proclaim this truth to others. Thus we seek to place ourselves under the authority of Scripture as we seek to live out a commitment to Jesus' lordship in our lives. Even though some issues and questions remain unanswered, we nevertheless affirm a completely inspired, truthful, and authoritative Bible with all its difficulties, rather than doubt. We accept the difficulties and humbly await the solution. But while we wait, with faith we stand on the Rock.

Conclusion

The Bible is the primary source of God's self-revelation for His people today. Even though times and cultures change, the basic needs shared by men and women of all ages and races in all times and cultures remain the same, and thus the message of God is normative, authoritative, and applicable as much for Christians in the twenty-first century as the first. We acknowledge that Scripture speaks to the spiritual needs of men and women, but more importantly it reveals the truth of and about God. We confess that all Scripture is inspired and is the true, reliable, Word of God for the people of God. Beyond these affirmations and articulations about the Word of God, we willingly and happily commit ourselves to it by placing our trust and confidence in the truthful, trustworthy, reliable, authoritative Word of God.

Further Reflection

1. What is at stake in the view we take of the Bible—its truthfulness and authority?
2. How do you view the Bible? What are your reasons for viewing it as you do?

For Additional Study

Dockery, David S. *Christian Scripture*. Nashville: Broadman & Holman, 1995.

Draper, James T. *Trusting Thy Word*. Nashville: Broadman, 1989.

The Triune God

The study of God is the fundamental doctrine of Christian theology. Some would suggest that the study of humankind or sinfulness is the proper starting point for doing theology. We would suggest, however, that humankind as creation is only understood in light of God as Creator and that sinfulness is understood only in light of God's holiness and grace (Isa. 6:1–8).

"We believe in God the Father Almighty, maker of Heaven and Earth"—The Apostle's Creed.

The biblical starting point brings us into the presence of God without delay. The biblical approach presupposes the existence of God and recognizes that only through special revelation is God truly revealed (Gen. 1:1). From this starting point the central affirmation of Scripture is not that there is a God but that God has acted and spoken in history.

Thinking about God

The Baptist Faith and Message confesses that "there is one and only one living and true God. He is an intelligent, spiritual, and personal being, the Creator, Redeemer, Preserver, and Ruler of the universe. God is infinite in holiness and all other perfections."

We confess our faith in the creating and redeeming God, but ultimately He cannot be exhaustively described or defined. Yet the following foundational principles can be helpful in our thinking about God:

"Listen, Israel: The LORD our God, the LORD is One. Love the LORD your God with all your heart, with all your soul, and with all your strength" (Deut. 6:4-5).

1. God has spoken to men and women, and the Bible is His Word, which has been given to us to make us wise unto salvation.

2. God is Lord and King over this world, ruling all things for His own glory, displaying His perfections in all that He does in order that humans and angels may worship and adore Him.

3. God is Savior, active in sovereign love through the Lord Jesus Christ to rescue believers from the guilt and power of sin, to adopt them as His children and accordingly to bless them.

4. God is Triune; there are within the Godhead three persons: the Father, Son, and Holy Spirit. And the work of salvation is one in which all three act together, purposing, providing, and applying forgiveness.

Godliness means responding to God's revelation in trust and obedience, faith and worship, prayer and praise, submission and service. True Christianity is seeing life and living it in light of God's written Word (adapted from J. I. Packer).

To think wrongly about God is idolatry (Ps. 50:21). Thinking rightly about God is eternal life (John 17:3) and should be the believer's life objective (Jer. 9:23–24). We can think rightly about God because He is knowable (1 Cor. 2:11), yet we must remain mindful that He is simultaneously incomprehensible (Rom. 11:33–36). God can be known, but He cannot be known completely (Deut. 29:29).

"This is eternal life: that they may know You, the only true God, and the One You have sent—Jesus Christ" (John 17:3).

Personal Nature of God

God is personal and is differentiated from other beings, nature, and the universe. This is in contrast to current philosophical approaches to God that say God is in a part of the world, creating a continual process, and the process itself is God. These approaches speak of God as being and becoming.

The Bible, however, proclaims God as Spirit (John 4:24), alive (Deut. 5:26), intelligent (Rom. 11:33), purposive (Eph. 1:11; 3:11), active (John 5:17), and free (Ps. 135:5–9). God is free in that His actions are determined *solely by His own nature and pleasure*. Only an absolutely free person can limit himself, and God has chosen to limit Himself. He cannot do anything prohibited by His own nature. As a personal God, He is self-conscious (Exod. 3:14), knowing Himself completely. He is emotional; yet these emotions, unlike human emotions, are not mixed with imperfections and weaknesses. We learn that God rejoices (Isa. 62:5), loves (Jer. 31:3), shows compassion (Ps. 145:8), demonstrates pity (Ps. 103:3), hates (Ps. 5:5), is jealous (Deut. 5:9), and can suffer and be grieved (Judg. 10:16).

The Attributes of God

When we talk about the attributes of God, we are affirming something true about God that has been revealed in creation, Scripture, or Christ. The study of the attributes of God, far from being boring, may, for God's people, be a sweet and absorbing spiritual exercise.

For the soul that is thirsty for God (Ps. 42:1), nothing could be more enjoyable or delightful.

Attributes of Greatness

Self-existent. When we confess that God is self-existent, we mean He is totally self-sufficient, depending on nothing external to Himself. The source of God's existence is completely within Himself (Ps. 36:9; John 5:26).

Infinite. We gladly affirm that God is infinite in relation to time, space, knowledge, and power. When we say God is infinite, we mean that God is not only unlimited but that nothing outside Himself can be a limit to Him.

God's infinity and time (eternity). God is eternal, and His existence is not measured by time. This does not mean that God is timeless but rather that He is above time or over time. We must acknowledge that He is aware of what has happened, what is happening, and what will happen at each point in time. He has from all eternity known what He is doing and will do (Ps. 139:7–12; Acts 17:24–25).

God's omniscience. God always acts with all the facts. His knowledge is all-inclusive (past, present, and future) and complete. He does not grow in knowledge (Ps. 147:4; Rom. 11:33).

God's omnipotence. God can do all things consistent with His nature. We confess biblical affirmations about God's power, not philosophical abstractions. God's energy is constant and never will be diminished. Where the Bible maintains that all things are possible (Matt. 19:6), it is primarily a confession about God's relation to people, although it also has reference to God's power over nature (Isa. 40:28; Jer. 32:15–17).

Sovereignty. God is the Supreme Being and Ruler in the universe, is total and absolute, and is in control of all things (Eph. 1:11).

Constant and Consistent. Some theologians refer to God's consistency as His immutability. We prefer to speak of God as consistent because immutability is often misunderstood as meaning immobility. An unchanging God must change or respond in His dealing with humanity (such as His negative response to Adam and His positive response to Nineveh) in order to remain unchangeable in His character (Num. 23:19; James 1:17). There is no change in God's nature, character, or purpose, though there are changes or responses

"God is light, and there is absolutely no darkness in Him" (1 John 1:5).

"God is love" (1 John 4:8).

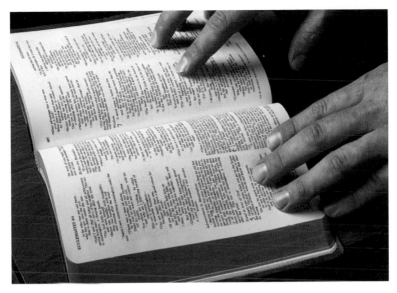

in His actions and dealings. To affirm that God is consistent means He never becomes greater, better, or worse; He never learns, grows, develops, improves, evolves, or gets younger or older. While He is consistent, He is not static or isolated from His creation but dynamic and involved with His creation. He does feel, sympathize, and express emotion and passion; but He does so perfectly and consistently.

The Bible teaches that God is immutable.

Attributes of Goodness

Holiness. To affirm that God is holy means He is both completely unique and absolutely pure. God is unique, separate from the ordinary sense of life. He is majestic in holiness. The expression of God's love is regulated by His holiness, and His holiness is related to His faithfulness and the surety of His covenants (Ps. 105:42; Num. 20:6–13). It is right to see God's holiness as a controlling attribute in relation to His other attributes of goodness (Isa. 6:1–4; 57:15; 1 Pet. 1:15–16).

Righteousness. God is absolutely right beyond all comprehension in reference to His law (Ps. 19:7–9), His actions (Gen. 18:25), and in His relationships. God's actions are right not just because He pronounces them right but because He acts consistently with His nature, thus His actions are objectively right.

Justice. The application of His righteousness and the administration of righteousness to others is God's justice. Because He is just, He must punish sin (Gen. 2:17; Rom. 6:3), which includes the exercise of His wrath (Rom. 1:18). Apparent injustices in society will be made right by God's eschatological justice (Ps. 73). But we, as God's people, are to seek justice in society (Amos 5:12–15; James 2:9).

Truth. God makes good His every word and promise (John 17:17–19). God can always be trusted. This assures us that He will respond to all true worship (John 4:24).

Faithfulness. God's faithfulness is closely related to His consistency. His will and actions are always found true, reliable, and steadfast. He will never commit Himself to do something He is not capable of doing (Lam. 3:23–24; 1 Thess. 5:24).

Love. God's love includes fatherly benevolence (Matt. 5:45), motherly care (Isa. 49:14–16), and a parental discipline (Heb. 12:6) because His love is a holy love. There is in God no thought of personal benefit since He seeks only the good of the ones loved (1 John 4:7–8) and does not wait for a reciprocal response to be expressed.

Grace. God deals with women and men on the basis of His goodness and generosity, not on any merit in us but according to our need. God could love unselfishly and insist that His love be deserved, but His grace requires absolutely nothing. Grace is giving us what we do not deserve (Eph. 1:7; 2:8; Titus 3:4–7). God is truly righteous and holy as well as truly loving and gracious.

Mercy. God is likewise tenderhearted and demonstrates loving compassion for His people (Exod. 3:7; Ps. 103:13). This includes His slowness toward anger and wrath which is His persistent love (Rom. 2:4; 2 Pet. 3:9). If grace is giving us what we do not deserve, God's mercy includes not giving us what we deserve. We can conclude that all of God's attributes work together. Between His attributes there are no contradictions. One attribute does not need to be suspended to demonstrate another. His attributes are not added together to make up His total being. Rather, in Him all His attributes are one. All of God does all that He does, and He does not divide Himself to act. He works in the complete unity of His being. Thus we can speak of His holy love. To see God for who He is gives believers a God-centered perspective of life and ministry. It also enables us to see theology not from the standpoint of the needs of men and women, which produces an inverted theology, but from the viewpoint of God's majestic glory (adapted from Millard Erickson. See *For Additional Study*).

The Triune God

Scripture reveals the unity of God (Deut. 6:4; Eph. 4:6; 1 Tim. 2:5). It also asserts or implies the deity of three Persons: Father (John 6:27), Son (Heb. 1:8), and Holy Spirit (Acts 5:3–4). Also the Bible pictures the Trinity in action at the birth (Luke 1:35) and baptism (Matt. 3:16) of Jesus. The Trinity is associated together in benedictions, doxologies, and baptismal formulas (Matt. 28:19–20; 2 Cor. 13:14).

We can say that God is one in His nature and three in His Persons. More specifically we can confess that there is only one God, but in the unity of the Godhead there are three eternal and coequal Persons, the same in substance yet distinct in function. The members of the Trinity are equal, yet they may functionally subordinate at times. Without the Trinity we have no final and perfect revelation of God. God is perfectly infinite, and only God can reveal God perfectly and adequately. Thus Christ perfectly reveals an infinite God to finite and imperfect humanity while the Spirit makes known to us the fullness of Christ.

The teaching regarding the Trinity is incomprehensible. It is truth for the heart. The fact that it cannot be completely explained is something we should have expected. A God who is understood completely is no God. No one could have imagined this doctrine; such a truth had to be revealed. As the church fathers affirmed, the Trinity

Because He is just, God must punish sin.

is divinely revealed, not humanly constructed. It would be absurd if it were a human invention. It is not self-evident, but it is a mystery that God has revealed.

Without the Trinity there could be no salvation from sin in the biblical sense. If there had been no Incarnation, there would have been no Savior. Without a Savior there would have been no atonement and no salvation for the Spirit to apply. All analogies to explain the Trinity fall short, resulting in functional understandings of the Trinity, resulting in either modalism or tritheism (one person manifesting himself in three ways or three different gods, respectively.) Try to explain it, and we might think we are losing our minds. Far worse, try to deny it, and we will lose our very souls.

Conclusion

God is not physical but spiritual, not dead but living, not passive but active, not impersonal but personal. As a personal Spirit, God has intellect, emotions, and will. He enjoys fellowship with persons created in His image. The Trinitarian God acts consistently with His nature; He cannot deny Himself. God is absolutely free, holy, loving, gracious, and infinitely wise in all He does. God has fully revealed Himself in the person and ministry of the Lord Jesus Christ (John 1:14, 18; 14:9).

A right response to these truths will create a God-centered life that focuses on the majesty and glory of God. God desires our worship in spirit and truth (John 4:24). He initiates a relationship with His creatures, and our worship is an encounter with God that only He can make possible by His grace.

Further Reflection
1. What difference does it make how we view God?
2. Why is the doctrine of the Trinity so important?

For Additional Study

Erickson, Millard J. *God the Father Almighty*. Grand Rapids: Baker, 1995.

Piper, John. *Desiring God*. Portland: Multnomah, 1986.

Tozer, A. W. *The Knowledge of the Holy*. New York: Harper, 1961.

Creation and Providence

Creation

We confess that God, without the use of any preexisting material, brought into being everything that is. Both the opening verse of the Bible and the initial sentence of the Apostle's Creed confess God as Creator. The theme of God as Creator of the heavens and earth is clearly taught in Scripture from beginning to end (Gen. 1:1; Isa. 40:28; Mark 13:19; Rev. 10:6). The Bible affirms that God is the direct Creator of men and women (Gen. 1:27; Mark 10:6), of His covenant people Israel (Isa. 43:15), and in fact of all things (Col. 1:16; Rev. 4:11). With Scripture we maintain that Creation occurred by God's Word (Gen. 1:3; Pss. 33:6–9; 148:5). The spoken word that brought Creation into being is vitally related to the eternal Word who was with

"In the beginning God created the heavens and the earth" (Gen. 1:1).

That God is Creator is clearly taught throughout Scripure.

God and who was God (John 1:1). According to John's Gospel (John 1:3), all things were made through the Word and without this Word nothing was made that was made. This Word was Jesus.

Creation is the work of the Trinitarian God (Gen. 1; Heb. 11:3). God the Father is the source of Creation (1 Cor. 8:6), the Son is the agent of Creation (Col. 1:16), and the Spirit of God was lovingly hovering over the work of Creation (Gen. 1:2). Creation was by the wisdom of God (Jer. 10:12), the will of God (Rev. 4:11), and, as previously noted, the Word of God (Ps. 33:6–9). Creation reveals God (Ps. 19:1) and brings glory to Him (Isa. 43:7). All of creation was originally good (Gen. 1:4, 31) but is now imperfect because of the entrance and effects of sin on creation (Gen. 3:16–19). This is, however, only a temporary imperfection (Rom. 8:19–22), for it will be redeemed in the final work of God, the new creation (Isa. 65; Rev. 21:15).

The biblical doctrine of Creation affirms God as Creator, Redeemer, and Ruler. The Creator God is not different from the God who works out our salvation in Jesus Christ through His Holy Spirit. God is the Source of all things. This means that God has brought the world into existence *out of nothing* through a purposeful act of His free will. We thus affirm God as the sovereign and almighty Lord of all existence. Such an affirmation rejects any form of dualism, that matter has eternally existed, that matter must, therefore, be evil since it is in principle opposed to God, the Source of all good.

The doctrine of Creation also maintains that God is set apart from and transcends His creation. It also maintains that God is a purposeful God who creates in freedom. In Creation and in God's provision and preservation for creation, He is working out His ultimate purposes for humanity and the world. Human life is thus meaningful, significant, intelligent, and purposeful. This affirms the overall unity and intelligibility of the universe. In this we see God's greatness, goodness, and wisdom. The Creation account finds its full explication in Jesus as the God-Man, the light and life of the world who will bring creation under His domain at the consummation of the world, leading to the ultimate praise and glory of the Creator God.

Preservation and Providence

The Baptist Faith and Message says, "God as Father reigns with providential care over His universe, His creatures, and the flow of the stream of human history according to the purposes of His grace."

Preservation. God's work of preservation includes His intervention into the affairs of history. This biblical affirmation of preservation must be distinguished from a deistic view of a distant God—one who doesn't interact with His creation. Yet God's work of maintaining and protecting the existence of the created universe is accomplished through the nature of His creative work and by His continuing providential care and intervention. In Colossians 1:16–17, the verb form (perfect tense) emphasizes the ongoing result of God's "holding together all things" (also Heb. 1:3).

Providence. Closely related, and even larger in scope, is God's work of providence. Providence involves the continuing work of the Triune God whereby all things in the universe are directed and controlled by God, thereby assuredly bringing about His wise plan (Rom. 8:28).

"Providence is God's own act by which God orders all events in creation, nature, and history, so that the ends for which God created them will be in due time realized. The final end is that all creatures will, in God's own time, manifest God's glory and reflect as they are capable the divine happiness"—Thomas C. Oden, *Systematic Theology,* Vol. I, 270.

God the Father is the source of Creation (1 Cor. 8:6).

This is carried out, generally, by the establishment and outworking of natural laws and principles that are part of God's good and wise creation. It can, however, also include God's unique, purposeful, and special intervention into the natural process to accomplish His will, which we refer to as a miracle. Miracles, while an aspect of God's providence, must be seen for their uniqueness.

God's providence at times also transcends the affairs of women and men. In so doing, God can take actions intended as evil and use them for His good (Gen. 50:20). Such work on the part of God can only bring a response of praise from believers for God's greatness. At the same time, this raises one of the most difficult questions in Christian theology: Why do evil and suffering continue in this world?

Some have proposed that God either does not exist or is not powerful enough to do anything about evil or is not loving enough to be concerned about suffering. In contrast to this, we want not only to

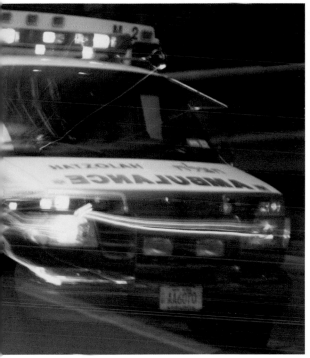

Some have proposed that God either does not exist or is not powerful enough to do anything about evil or is not loving enough to be concerned about suffering.

confess that God exists but also that He is indeed infinitely powerful and absolutely loving. Yet we do not want to deny evil and suffering either, for it is obviously present around us.

Ultimately we answer this question by confessing that God has a plan and a purpose and puts all things into perspective (Eccl. 9:11). Evil still exists because Satan, a completely evil creature, exists and continually opposes and attempts to thwart the plan of God. God allows evil to exist to further and broaden God's revelation (Ps. 107:28). Apart from sin, evil, and suffering, God's love, mercy, and grace are not fully revealed. God also uses suffering to bring about discipline or punishment among His creatures. Evil does exist, but it has not always existed, and it will be removed from the new creation when God's plan of the ages is brought to completion.

Finally, we must confess our limited knowledge at this point and say that the problem of evil remains a mystery. We can, with

"If God is well pleased so long as we do not deny His ordinances, what supreme pleasure we must afford Him when we accept His will with cheerfulness in sufferings that touch our own person. . . . Afflictions and the cauterization of the flesh burn away the rust of sin and perfect the life of the just" — Anselm of Canterbury.

scriptural affirmation, be assured that God can and does use sin, evil, failure, and suffering for His eternal good. The ultimate example is the crucifixion of Christ, which pictures Christ in His suffering state because of the sinful, evil actions of humanity. Yet through the triumph of the Resurrection, the greatest act of evil (the crucifixion of the God-Man Jesus Christ) became the greatest good, the provision of forgiveness of sin, and the salvation of humankind. All of this points to God's wise and wonderful plan for this world, part of which has been revealed to us but which is finally incomprehensible in its totality to God's creatures.

The Plan of God

Perhaps prior to a discussion of God's creative acts and His providential oversight is an understanding of God's plan. This refers to the consistent and coherent intention of God's will, an eternal decision rendering certain all things that will come to pass. God's plan not only relates to His creatures, men and women, as moral agents but also to any and all matters in the realm of cosmic history.

God is a loving covenant God who cares for and sustains His people. For Old Testament believers it was almost inconceivable that anything could happen independently of God's plan and the outworking of it. The Hebrew Scripture does not say the rains came and then the sun began to shine but that God sent the rains and then caused the sun to shine. Throughout it reveals God's faithfulness in bringing about and directing His plan in history as well as the futility of opposing it (Isa. 46:10–11; Prov. 19:21).

God's plan is from all eternity (Eph. 3:11). Nothing in time catches God by surprise and causes Him to seek a contingency plan. God's plan is free and purposive (Eph. 1:11–14); it is for His good pleasure (Rev. 4:11). The plan, as with all of God's thoughts and acts, is always consistent with His nature. Also God's plan is effective but does not force His creatures to act in a certain way. Yet the plan of God renders it certain that they will freely act in the ways they so choose. When discussing the plan of God, it is important not to emphasize the sovereignty of God over His other attributes. Ultimately the plan of God is for His own glory (Eph. 1:6, 12, 18; Rev. 4:11); it exalts God (Ps. 29:1–2) and affirms that God is in control of the events of history (Acts 4:23–28).

> "A deistic God whose creation was a self-running machine might have to wrench the works of his machine for this purpose; but the God of biblical theism is continually active in upholding the drama of his universe, and can interact with his creatures through law-like as well as unprecedented turns of events"—Donald M. MacKay, *Science, Chance, and Providence* (Oxford: Oxford University Press, 1978), 64.

Angels, Satan, and Demons

Angels. Angels are God's messengers, powerful beings that inhabit the heavenly spheres. The angels were present to praise God at Creation as implied by Job 38:6–7 and Psalm 148:2–5. They were created good because God cannot create anything evil. Angels, as free moral agents, are responsible for their actions and may choose evil rather than obedience (Matt. 25:41).

Ultimately the plan of God is for His own glory (Eph. 1:6, 12, 18; Rev. 4:11).

Discerning Demons

"How can we tell that we are dealing with demonic agents when many of their characteristic strategies employ the temptations, doubts, lies and slanders common to the flesh and the world? There is a simple response to this question. The powers of darkness do not afflict us aimlessly. There is usually design in their operations, and the design centers on blocking the expansion of the Messianic kingdom. Much of our discernment of Satanic powers comes as we follow the Holy Spirit's guidance in mission and ministry. As we begin initiatives for the kingdom, events will turn in a direction precisely calculated to block our efforts. These events will often be enveloped in a cloud of lies, accusations and misunderstandings, which is the devil's native atmosphere. If all this comes with an especially disabling power behind it, Satan is probably involved"—Richard F. Lovelace, *Renewal as a Way of Life* (InterVarsity Press, 1985), 153–54.

Angels are intelligent beings evidencing understanding (Matt. 18:10) and curiosity (1 Pet. 1:12). As emotional beings they are capable of praise (Luke 2:13–14), rejoicing (Luke 15:10), and anger (Rev. 12). They are volitional beings who can plan (Jude 9) and choose to sin (2 Pet. 2:4); thus they are also responsible for their actions (Matt. 25:41; Jude 6). Angels are creatures who do not create, marry, or propagate (Mark 12:25). As spirit beings, they serve those who will inherit salvation (Heb. 1:14). They are immortal (Luke 20:36) and are innumerable (Job 38:7; Rev. 12:4).

The Bible classifies angels into elect angels and fallen or none-lect angels (Mark 8:38; Matt. 25:41). Apparently some of these are already bound (2 Pet. 2:4), though perhaps some, as demons, are loose (Matt. 12:22). The elect angels have forms of organization including archangels (Michael, Dan. 10:13), thrones, dominions, principalities, authorities, powers, cherubim, seraphim, and living creatures. It is difficult to know the full meaning of these distinctions or if there is some hierarchy among them beyond the archangel. These angels bring revelation (Dan. 9:21–22), strengthen and minister to God's people (Heb. 1:14), protect (Matt. 2:13), and dispense judgments (Rev. 8; 9; 16). Angels were present at primary events of revelation and redemption such as Creation (Job 38:7), the giving of the Law (Gal. 3:19), the birth of Christ (Matt. 1:20), and the inauguration of the church (Acts 1:10). They will be present during Christ's reign (Rev. 20).

Satan and Demons. The devil is a high angelic creature who before the creation of the human race rebelled against the Creator and became the chief antagonist of God and humankind. At the time of Satan's fall, many angels (demons) fell with him. As mentioned above, some of these roam free while others are bound.

Satan is an intelligent and powerful being. His power extends not only over the angelic realm (Matt. 25:41) but is also exerted in the physical realm of men and women (2 Cor. 12:7), in their hearts and thoughts (Matt. 16:23), in government (John 12:31), in the spiritual realm (Matt. 13:19), in the church (1 Tim. 4:1), and even in death (Job 1:19). Scripture gives numerous titles and pictures of Satan (2 Cor. 11:3–4; 1 Pet. 5:8–9; Rev. 12:3–4). These titles and pictures describe Satan as a murderer and a liar (John 8:44) who violates the sacredness of life and truth, a sinner (1 John 3:8), an accuser of the saints (Rev. 12:10), and extremely prideful (1 Tim. 3:6). While

Satan, as a powerful being, is active in these areas, it is important to remember that he is accountable (Matt. 25:41) and does not have infinite knowledge (Job 1:7) or power (Rev. 20). Thus, he can be resisted (Eph. 6:10–17; James 4:7).

Satan's activities include counterfeiting (2 Cor. 11:14–15), slandering (Gen. 3:4–5), deceiving (Rev. 20:3), attempting to destroy the work of Jesus (1 John 3:8), blinding (2 Cor. 4:4), and accusing believers (Rev. 12:10). Also he hinders ministry (1 Thess. 2:18), incites persecution (Rev. 2:10), and tempts to sin (Acts 5:3). The purpose of Satan is not primarily to establish a kingdom of crime and confusion but to establish a permanent kingdom that supplants and coexists with God's kingdom. In so doing, he focuses attention upon the minds of human beings whom he tempts to doubt the existence of God, and if not that, the goodness of God. He presents attractive counterfeits for God's will and true worship such as false piety, religious practices, money, power, and prestige. One of Satan's greatest ploys is to fix our attention on the present instead of God's eternal values (Matt. 4:1–11).

Believers should respond with total dependence on the Lord Jesus Christ. One should not overestimate or underestimate Satan's tactics. Instead, members of the community of faith must draw upon the spiritual resources available to them, stand firm, ultimately submit to God, resist the devil, and draw near to God. God will in turn draw near to His people (James 4:7–8).

Conclusion

God, as the transcendent Lord of all space and time, is not indebted to the world or bound to it. God does not need this universe in order to be God. The world depends on God for its origin, unity, and continuity. God, who is Creator, is also Redeemer and Ruler, and He sustains the world as Preserver by His providential care. Such a view of providence shows history moving toward its consummation in the purposes of the Creator. God's purposes in the world are being realized through the general laws of nature, historical events, the actions of humans, as well as special times of gracious intervention.

God's plan is purposeful, effectual, and pleasing to God. There are invisible spiritual beings (angels, Satan, and demons) that influence God's world both for good and for evil either as God's ministering spirits (angels) or God's opponents, attempting to usurp the kingdom of God (Satan and demons). Even though there is evil in the world, God's goodness will ultimately triumph over evil, and His providential care can take that which was intended for evil and use it for good, advancing the kingdom of God and bringing eternal glory to the name of God. We take comfort and encouragement in these important truths related to God's providential care and direction for this world (His creation) and for us (His creatures).

Further Reflection

1. How should our praying be impacted by our understanding of God's providential plan?
2. What place do angels play in our daily lives and spiritual maturity?

For Additional Study

Berkouwer, G. C. *The Providence of God*. Grand Rapids: Eerdmans, 1952.

Bray, Gerald. *The Doctrine of God*. InterVarsity: Downers Grove, 1993.

Dickason, C. Fred. *Angels, Elect and Evil*. Chicago: Moody, 1975.

The Person of Jesus Christ

Jesus Christ, who was eternally the second Person of the Trinity sharing all the divine attributes, became fully human. In entering the world as a human, Jesus took on human characteristics while voluntarily choosing to exercise His divine powers only intermittently in order to fulfill His redemptive mission. The biblical writers indicate who Jesus is by describing the significance of the work He came to do and the office He came to fulfill.

The Person of Jesus Christ

When we point to Jesus, we see the whole man Jesus and say that He is God. This man Jesus Christ does not only live through God and with God, but He is Himself God. The confession of the Christian church has maintained Christ as one Person having two natures, the one divine and the other human. This is the great mystery of godliness, God manifested in the flesh (1 Tim. 3:16).

The Humanity of Jesus

Jesus' humanity is taken for granted in the Synoptic Gospels. But in other parts of the New Testament, it seems to be witnessed to in particular as if it might have been called into question or its significance neglected (1 John 1:12; 4:23). In Mark's Gospel there is concentration on the humanity of Jesus as much as in any New Testament book. Matthew and Luke focus on Jesus' birth stories as aspects of His humanity, including the temptation accounts. John pictures Jesus as the eternal Word who took on full humanity (John 1:1, 14; 4:6–7; 11:33–35). He is a real man yet sinless and different from other humans (Rom. 8:3). His significance is not found through comparison alongside others but in contrast with others (Heb. 2:9, 14–18; 5:7–8; 10:10). This uniqueness is especially seen in His miraculous birth and sinless life.

"It is also taught among us that God the Son became man, born of the Virgin Mary, and that the two natures, divine and human, are so inseparably united in one person that there is one Christ, true God and true man"—Article III, The Augsburg Confession, 1530.

"For a child will be born to us, a son will be given to us; And the government will rest on His shoulders; And His name will be called Wonderful Counselor, Mighty God, Eternal Father, Prince of Peace" (Isa. 9:6, NASB).

Virgin Birth. The birth of Jesus resulted from a miraculous conception. He was conceived in the womb of the virgin Mary by the power of the Holy Spirit without male seed (Matt. 1:18–25; Luke 1:26–38). This does not in any way teach Mary's continual virginity.

While the biblical writers do not amplify upon the theological significance of the birth of Christ, such significance cannot be overlooked. God's deliverance has come, and it calls to mind a sign (Isa. 7:14) of God's great Old Testament promises. The unique birth affirms Jesus' true humanity and His deity. It reveals that Jesus was really born, really one of us, but that this birth was a supernatural event.

The Sinlessness of Jesus. The Gospels present Jesus as participating in John's baptism, which was a baptism of repentance. Also we see Jesus rebuking Peter, cleansing the Temple, confronting the Pharisees, and sending pigs into the sea. Jesus was baptized not for repentance from sin but in order to fulfill all righteousness and to identify completely with fallen humanity. The other examples are pictures of righteous anger, not sinful anger (see Eph. 4:26). The Bible carefully confesses the sinlessness of Jesus (Rom. 8:3; 2 Cor. 5:21; Heb. 4:15; 1 Pet. 2:22). The Bible stresses the true emptying of Jesus in becoming like us (Phil. 2:5–8), His full humanity, the reality of the temptations, His Spirit-enabled rejection of the temptations, and His resulting sinlessness.

The Deity of Jesus
Titles of Jesus Christ

"The Virgin Birth is the divinely ordered method of the incarnation of God in Jesus Christ, an essential historical indication of the Incarnation"—Carl F. H. Henry, "Our Lord's Virgin Birth," *Christianity Today*, 4:20.

The Gospels contain two classes of titles: those that go back to Jesus Himself and those that are applied to Him by others. There is considerable scholarly discussion about the exact nature of the first group, but the evidence of Scripture must be allowed to speak for itself. Jesus used certain titles for Himself and allowed His followers to refer to Him in certain ways. From these we gain insight into how He understood Himself and His mission.

Son of David. Son of David is a messianic title frequently used to refer to Jesus in the Gospels (Matt. 1:1; 9:27; 15:22; 20:30–31; 21:9, 15). The title expresses hope. The Son of David, who was greater than David (22:41–45), would bring deliverance for those hopelessly in bondage.

Son of Man. This was Jesus' favorite self-designation. It originated in the Old Testament (Dan. 7:13–14), was used during the intertes-

Opposite:
A sculpture of the ʰoly family from ᵉzareth

tamental period, and was chosen by Jesus to define His messianic mission. It was used because it had messianic overtones. The idea of messiahship current in His day was that of a military hero, whereas He came to be the Savior of the world.

Jesus used the title *Son of Man* in four different ways. First, frequently it was a synonym for "I." Jesus was simply referring to Himself (for example, see Matt. 26:24). Second, the Son of Man is one who exercises divine authority (for example, see Matt. 9:6). Third, the Son of Man fulfills His earthly mission by death and Resurrection (for example, see Matt. 12:40; 17:9, 12, 23). Fourth, the Son of Man will return in great glory to establish His kingdom (for example, see Matt. 16:27–28; 19:28). In this way Jesus defined who He, the messianic Son of Man, is.

Son, Son of God, Only Son. The title *Son of God*, or *Son* for short, was also a messianic title derived from the Old Testament (2 Sam. 7:11–16). It assumes a more exalted status, however, when used by or about Jesus. It means in fact that Jesus possesses the qualities of the divine nature. This was quite evident when the heavenly voice cried out to Jesus at His baptism that He was beloved and well pleasing (Matt. 3:16–17), an affirmation reiterated at Jesus' Transfiguration (Mark 9:7).

Jesus' own understanding of His unique relation to God as Son is reflected in Matthew 11:25–27 and Luke 10:21–22. Jesus expressed the same idea when confounding the Pharisees (Matt. 22:41–46). In the Gospel of John, Jesus is referred to as God's "one and only Son" (John 3:16), a term that means *one of a kind or unique.*

Holy One of God. This is a term used specifically by supernatural evil beings of Jesus as the one who is pure and holy (Mark 1:24; Luke 4:34; John 6:69). As such He sealed their doom in that He is wholly righteous and they are wholly evil. It identified Jesus with the Holy God (compare to Isa. 6).

Savior. It is self-evident in the Old Testament that just as there is only one God, so there is only one Savior (for example, see Isa. 43:3, 11; 45:21). This is also true in the New Testament (1 Tim. 2:3; 4:10; Titus 1:3, 2:10). It is all the more significant, then, that Jesus is announced as the Savior of Israel (Luke 2:11) and the world (John 4:42) in the Gospels. Jesus was understood to be divine redemption incarnate and was proclaimed as such by the early church (Acts 5:31; 13:23; 1 John 4:14).

66

"Jesus Christ, true God, begotten of the Father from eternity, and also true man, born of the Virgin Mary, is my Lord"—Martin Luther, *Small Catechism.*

99

Jesus as the Word of God supremely reveals who God is.

The Word. In the Gospels this title is found only in John (1:1–14) The expression "Word of God" is common in both the Old and New Testaments as defining how God expressed Himself and what the content of that communication was. When referring to Jesus, it makes that self-revelation of God personal. Jesus as the Word of God supremely reveals who God is. If we would know God, we are to look at Jesus, the very expression (Word) of God. "Anyone who has seen me has seen the Father" (John 14:9), said Jesus.

Christ (Messiah). Jesus was reluctant to acknowledge this title because of the popular misconceptions that abounded about the Messiah, centering on a political king to rule on David's throne. Under the proper circumstances, however, He was willing to confess that He was indeed God's Anointed One (Matt. 16:13–20; 26:62–64; John 4:25–26). This title was used so commonly later on in the church that it virtually became a name for Jesus; so "Jesus the Christ" became simply "Christ."

"In the beginning was the Word, and the Word was with God, and the Word was God.... The Word became flesh and took up residence among us. We observed His glory, the glory as the One and Only Son from the Father, full of grace and truth" (John 1:1, 14).

"Long ago God spoke to the fathers by the prophets at different times and in different ways. In these last days, He has spoken to us by [His] Son, whom He has appointed heir of all things and through whom He made the universe" (Heb. 1:1-2).

Lord. This was a title of honor used of Jesus, the equivalent of "Master" or "Sir." However, we can see in it something of greater significance (Matt. 8:5–13; Mark 2:23–27). In Judaism "Lord" had become the word pronounced when the personal name Yahweh appeared in Scripture. "Lord" thus meant God. The church later, in light of Jesus' death and Resurrection, used it to mean nothing less than that Jesus was God.

God in Human Form

Paul affirmed that Jesus existed in the form of God from all eternity past (Phil. 2:5–11). This means Jesus possessed inwardly and demonstrated outwardly the very nature of God Himself (Col. 1:15–16; 2:9). Also the opening verse of John's Gospel is a categorized affirmation of Jesus' full deity (John 1:12; 14:9; 17:5). Pictures of Jesus' deity also are in the unique "I am" statements of John's Gospel (John 6:35; 8:12; 10:7–9, 11–14; 11:25; 14:6; 15:1–5). We see this particularly in Jesus' statement about His eternal existence that comes during the confrontation with the Jews (John 8:58). Finally, we see Jesus receiving the worship of Thomas (John 20:28) in his confession, "My Lord and my God." These passages, along with others in the New Testament (see Rom. 9:5; Titus 2:13; Heb. 1:1–8) cut across all lesser confessions of Christ's person, showing that any view that would make Him merely a great teacher or a great prophet is not adequate.

The *I Ams* of John's Gospel

I am the bread of life *6:35-48*
I am the living bread *6:51*
I am the light of the world *8:12*
I am from above; I am not of this world *8:23*
I am the gate for the sheep *10:7*
I am the good shepherd *10:11*
I am the resurrection and the life *11:25*
I am the way, and the truth, and the life *14:6*
I am the true vine *15:1*

Unity of the Two Natures

It is necessary that Christ should be both God and man. Only as a man could He be the Redeemer for humanity; only as a sinless man could He fittingly die for others. Only as God could His life, ministry, and redeeming death have infinite value and satisfy the demands of God so as to deliver others from death.

Christ has a human nature, but He is not merely a human person. The person of Christ is the God-Man, the second person of the Trinity. In the Incarnation He did not change into a human person or adopt a human personage. He assumed a human nature in addition to His eternal divine nature. With the assumption of the human nature,

"Following, then the holy fathers, we unite in teaching all men to confess the one and only Son, our Lord Jesus Christ. This selfsame one is perfect both in deity and also in humanness; this selfsame one is also actually God and actually man, with a rational soul and a body. He is of the same reality as God as far as His deity is concerned and of the same reality as we are ourselves as far as His humanness is concerned; thus like us in all respects, sin only excepted"—The Definition of Chalcedon, 451.

A sculptor's interpretation of Jesus the healer

He is not a divine person or a human person but a divine-human person possessing all the essential qualities of both the human and divine nature. This is a mystery beyond full comprehension. Also it is confessed that Jesus has both a divine and human consciousness as well as a human and divine will, yet clearly a unity of person. He is always the same person, Jesus Christ the Lord.

We affirm the uniqueness of Jesus and the exalted view of Him by the early church. The total impression gained after reflecting upon the attributes of Jesus and their significance is that Jesus was recognized in His person as fully God and fully human.

● "Only God himself, taking on human flesh and dying and rising in our flesh can effect a redemption that consists in being saved from sin, death, and corruption, and in being raised to share the nature of God himself"—*Council of Nicea*, 325.

● "The unassumed is the unredeemed, therefore Jesus is true man and true God"—*Council of Constantinople*, 381.

● "A unity of the two natures in Christ's person so complete that the impassible Word can be said to have suffered death. The humanity of Christ was complete and entire, but had no independent subsistence"—*Council of Ephesus*, 431.

● "Christ in two natures united in one person without confusion, without conversion, without division, without separation"—*Council of Chalcedon*, 451.

● "Christ is the eternal Son of God. In His incarnation as Jesus Christ He was conceived of the Holy Spirit and born of the virgin Mary. Jesus perfectly revealed and did the will of God, taking upon Himself the demands and necessities of human nature and identifying Himself completely with mankind yet without sin"—*Baptist Faith and Message*, 1963.

Jesus knew and clearly announced who He was. His humanity veiled His deity as well as revealed His glory. He is the Suffering Servant as well as the eternal God. We confess our belief in Jesus the Christ, the Founder and Foundation of the Christian faith, one person, two natures. Our love for Him and our belief in Him must be matched by our worship of Him. He is the "Jesus loves me" of the children's song and the "Holy, Holy, Holy" of the great hymn.

"Christ, by highest heav'n adored, Christ, the everlasting Lord; Late in time, behold Him come, offspring of a virgin's womb. Veiled in flesh the Godhead see, Hail the incarnate Deity! Pleased as man with men to dwell, Jesus our Immanuel" —Charles Wesley, "Hark! The Herald Angels Sing."

Further Reflection

1. Can you imagine the impression of those around Jesus as they observed Him from day to day?
2. Why did Jesus evoke such hostility from many of the people who knew Him?

For Additional Study

Erickson, Millard J. *The Word Became Flesh*. Grand Rapids: Baker, 1991.

Henry, Carl F. H. *The Identity of Jesus of Nazareth*. Nashville: Broadman & Holman, 1992.

Wells, David F. *The Person of Christ*. Westchester, IL: Crossway, 1984.

The Work of Jesus Christ

"Yet He Himself bore our sicknesses, and He carried our pains; but we in turn regarded Him stricken, struck down by God, and afflicted. But He was pierced because of our transgressions, crushed because of our iniquities; punishment for our peace was on Him, and we are healed by His wounds" (Isa. 53:4-5).

"For God so loved the world, that he gave his only begotten Son" (John 3:16, KJV).

"For he hath made him to be sin for us, who knew no sin; that we might be made the righteousness of God in him" (2 Cor. 5:21, KJV).

The Work of Christ

Christ's life and death exemplified divine love and exerted an influence for good by providing a model of servanthood and sacrifice. But, more importantly, Christ's death provided for sinners a sinless substitutionary sacrifice that satisfies divine justice, an incomprehensibly valuable redemption delivering sinners from estrangement to full fellowship and inheritance in the household of God. In this lesson we shall look at the cross of Christ primarily from the viewpoint of atonement, redemption, reconciliation, and justification.

Atonement. The idea of atonement is the focal point of the New Testament idea of the saving work of Christ (Isa. 53:10; Rom. 3:25; 1 John 2:2; 4:10; Heb. 2:17). This understanding of Christ's work on the cross has reference to the effecting of satisfaction on God while effecting the same satisfaction on the guilt of sin. Atonement can only be rightly understood in light of the holiness and justice of God, the severity of the reaction of God's holiness to sin. This concept affirms that God's holiness must be satisfied and the sins of humanity must be removed.

Atonement is realized when God Himself takes upon Himself, in the person of Jesus, the sinfulness and guilt of humankind so that His justice might be executed and the sins of men and women forgiven. It is mandatory to underscore this idea by affirming that God is moved to this self-sacrifice by His infinite compassion.

Redemption. The idea of redemption is vitally related to the themes of liberation, deliverance, and ransom. Within this model a struggle is seen between the kingdom of God and the hostile powers enslaving humankind.

Redemption is the idea of bringing sinners out of such hostile

Christ's death provided for sinners a sinless substitutionary sacrifice that satisfies divine justice.

"It pleased God, in His eternal purpose, to choose and ordain the Lord Jesus, His only begotten Son, to be the mediator between God and man, the Prophet, Priest, and King"—Chapter VIII, The Westminster Confession, 1646.

"As Christ alone died for us, so He is also to be adored as the only Mediator and Advocate between God the Father and us"—Article 6, The Ten Conclusions of Berne, 1528.

bondage into authentic freedom (Col. 2:15). As Redeemer Jesus breaks the power of sin and creates a new and obedient heart by delivering us from the power of sin, guilt, death, and Satan, thus bringing about a people who have been bought with a price (1 Pet. 1:18).

Reconciliation. Reconciliation involves bringing fallen humanity out of alienation into a state of peace and harmony with God. Jesus, as Reconciler, heals the separation and brokenness created by sin and restores communion between God and humankind.

Reconciliation is not a process by which men and women become ever more acceptable to God but an act by which we are delivered from estrangement to fellowship with God. Because of Christ's work on the cross, God has chosen to treat men and women in sin as children rather than transgressors (2 Cor. 5:18–20; Eph. 2:12–16; Col. 1:20–22).

Throughout church history Christian thinkers emphasized some or all of these ideas, including some and rejecting others. It is important to see that all of these ideas, as well as the example Jesus provided for us (1 Pet. 2:21), are necessary. Other religions have a martyr, but Jesus' death was that of a Savior. It brings salvation from sins for men and women as Christ took our place and died our death. In this His work on the cross was substitutionary.

By His obedient life He fulfilled the law for us, and by His death on the cross He satisfied the demands of the law for us. The cross of Christ is the actual execution of justice of God's penalty revealed in the law (Gal. 3:10–13). This means that Christ suffered for our sins (2 Cor. 5:21). In Jesus, God's holy love is clearly demonstrated (1 John 4:10). Therefore we cannot rightfully understand the cross unless we perceive both God's anguish over sin and His infinite holiness that refuses to tolerate sin.

Justification. Justification is a Pauline concept, though it is found in other biblical writers, especially Luke. Justification is accomplished at the cross of Christ (Rom. 5:10), guaranteed by His Resurrection (Rom. 4:24–25), and applied to us when we believe (Rom. 5:1). Justification is a declaration of our righteousness. Experientially we still sin, but God views us as totally righteous, clothed in the robes of our Lord Jesus (Rom. 4:18). Because of Christ's sacrifice, God no longer counts our sins against us (2 Cor. 5:19–21). Justification is more than pardon; it is a granting of positive favor in God's sight (Rom. 3:21–26).

Garden of
Gethsemane,
Jerusalem

The Resurrection of Christ

The Resurrection is the core of the Christian message (1 Cor. 15:3–4). Paul said that if Jesus were not raised from death, the gospel would be without meaning (Luke 24:45–48; Acts 2:27, 35). The Resurrection is the public evidence God gave that Jesus is who He claimed to be.

Also it establishes Jesus' lordship and deity as well as the justification of sinners, which was accomplished at the cross (Rom. 1:3–4; 4:24–25). The Resurrection provides promise as well as guarantee of final judgment.

It promises that believers can be accepted by God, live a life pleasing to God, and have assurance of victory over death (1 Cor. 15:55–57). On the other hand, it is a pledge of God's final judgment for those who reject Christ as Lord and Savior (Acts 17:31).

> "
>
> "For it behooves Him, if He is a bridegroom, to take upon Himself the things which are His bride's, and to bestow upon her the things that are His. For if He gives her His body and His very self, how shall He not give her all that is His? And if He takes the body of the bride, how shall He not take all that is hers? . . . He by the wedding-ring of faith shares in the sins, death and pains of hell which are His bride's, nay, make them His own, and acts as if they were His own, and as if He Himself had sinned"—Martin Luther, *Christian Liberty*, quoted in Thomas C. Oden's *Systematic Theology*, Vol II, 395.
>
> "

**Garden tomb,
Jerusalem**

"If Christ has not been raised, then our preaching is without foundation, and so is your faith. In addition, we are found to be false witnesses about God, because we have testified about God that He raised up Christ—whom He did not raise up if in fact the dead are not raised. For if the dead are not raised, Christ has not been raised. And if Christ has not been raised, your faith is worthless; you are still in your sins. Therefore those who have fallen asleep in Christ have also perished. If we have placed our hope in Christ for this life only, we should be pitied more than anyone" (1 Cor. 15:14-19).

The Ascension and Exaltation of Christ

Following the Resurrection, Christ ascended into heaven (Acts 1:9–11), where He is exalted at God's right hand (Heb. 1:3), a position of honor. Having sat down, Christ demonstrates that His cross work is finished. His position at God's right hand signifies His sharing in God's rule and dominion and the power and authority to which He is entitled.

At God's right hand Jesus exercises His priesthood, interceding for His own (John 17; Rom. 8:34; Heb. 7:25). Here He serves as the defense advocate (1 John 2:1) of His church, over which He is head (Eph. 1:20–21). From here He will return to consummate God's redemptive plan.

"He honored the divine law by His personal obedience, and in His death on the cross He made provision for the redemption of men from sin. He was raised from the dead with a glorified body and appeared to His disciples as the person who was with them before His crucifixion.

He ascended into heaven and is now exalted at the right hand of God where He is the One Mediator, partaking of the nature of God and of man, and in whose Person is effected the reconciliation between God and man. He will return in power and glory to judge the world and to consummate His redemptive mission. He now dwells in all believers as the living and ever present Lord"—Baptist Faith and Message, 1963.

Conclusion

We trustingly confess and affirm that Jesus Christ as the God-Man has fully revealed God to men and women. Having lived a sinless life, Christ died in our place for our sins. He now sits exalted at God's right hand, a position of honor and exaltation, exercising His rule and dominion. We gladly acknowledge Jesus as Lord, our Prophet, Priest, and King, who has completely revealed God, reconciled humankind with God, and who sits enthroned as ruler of God's kingdom and head of His church. In Him we place our trust and hope, offering our thanksgiving for the salvation He has provided for us.

Further Reflection

1. Why was Jesus' sacrificial death required to atone for the sins of human beings?
2. How important is the Resurrection to the gospel?

For Additional Study

Erickson, Millard J. *The Word Became Flesh*. Grand Rapids: Baker, 1991.

Henry, Carl F. H. ed. *Jesus of Nazareth: Savior and Lord*. Grand Rapids: Eerdmans, 1966.

____ _____. *The Identity of Jesus*. Nashville: Broadman & Holman, 1992.

Leon Morris. *The Cross in the New Testament*. Grand Rapids: Eerdmans, 1965.

John R. W. Stott. *The Cross of Christ*. Downers Grove, Ill.: InterVarsity, 1986.

66

"Rudolph Bultmann, 'the father of demythologizing,' said that 'if the bones of the dead Jesus were discovered tomorrow in a Palestinian tomb, all the essentials of Christianity would remain unchanged.' Paul disagreed"—Peter Kreeft and Ronald K Tacelli, *Handbook of Christian Apologetics* (Downers Grove, Ill.: InterVarsity Press, 1994), 176.

99

Salvation

Men and women are the highest forms of God's earthly creation. All other aspects of creation are for the purpose of serving men and women; men and women are created to serve God and are thus theocentric. In this chapter we will discuss the subjects of humankind, their fall into sin, and God's salvation of men and women from their estranged, guilty, and dreadful plight.

Humankind
The Position and Nature of Humanity
Men and women are complex creatures of God composed of not only a physical body but also an immaterial self, called a *soul* or *spirit*. In the present life men and women function as whole persons, though it is a type of conditional unity because the material and immaterial aspects interact upon each other in such intricate ways that they are not easily distinguished. Yet as has been expounded by many in the history of the church, the characteristics of the immaterial (soul/spirit) cannot be attributed only to the physical. They remain distinct but not separated until death, closely related and interacting with each other. Humans were a unity at creation and will again be a complete unity at glorification, but during the present time we can affirm a type of conditional unity brought about by the entrance and effects of sin. The primary reason for the importance of men and women in creation, over against the rest of God's creation, is related to their creation in God's image (Gen. 1:26–27).

"Then God said, 'Let Us make man in Our image, according to Our likeness. They will rule the fish of the sea, the birds of the sky, the livestock, all the earth, and the creatures that crawl on the earth' So God created man in His own image; He created him in the image of God; He created them male and female" (Gen. 1:27-28).

The Image of God
God has created us in His image and likeness. At first this might appear to refer to our physical makeup—that we *look* like God. That is not what the Bible means by the terms "image and likeness

Men and women are the highest forms of God's earthly creation.

of God." Men and women, because they are created in the image of God, have rationality, morality, spirituality, and personality. They can relate to God and other humans while rightly exercising dominion over the earth and the animals (Gen. 1:26–28; Ps. 8).

Nothing in us or about us is separable, distinct, or discoverable as the divine image. Each person individually and the entire race corporately are the image of God. But no single aspect of human nature or behavior or thought pattern can be isolated as the image of God.

Male and Female

In creation there is a complete equality between men and women; neither sex is given prominence over the other. Again this is related to the fact that male and female are both created in God's image. Also "in Christ" in our redeemed state there is neither male nor female (Gal. 3:28). We cannot, however, bypass the teaching that a distinction between the roles or functions carried out by men and women is addressed in Genesis 2:18–25.

Sin and the Fall

Even though men and women are created in God's image, the entrance of sin into the world has had great and negative influences upon God's creation, especially humans, created in God's image. As a result of sin, the image of God was not lost (Gen. 9:6; James 3:9) but was severely tarnished and marred. The role of exercising dominion (Gen. 1:28) has been drastically disturbed by the effects of sin on humans and the curse on nature. The ability to live in right relationship with God, with others, with nature, and with our very own selves has been corrupted. All attempts at righteousness are as filthy rags in God's sight (Isa. 64:6), and humans are ultimately spiritually dead and alienated from God (Eph. 2:1–3). Therefore we are unable to reflect properly the divine image and likeness (Rom. 1:18–32).

It is necessary to see that the sin of Adam and Eve (Gen. 3) was not just a moral lapse but a deliberate turning away from God and rejection of Him. The day that they disobeyed God, they died spiritually—which ultimately brought physical death (Gen. 2:17). The consequences were many as Paul described in Romans 1:18; 3:20; 5:12–21; and Ephesians 2:1–22. Important among these consequences are the effects upon our wills, the volitional elements of men and women. Sin's entrance has brought about a sinful nature in all humanity. People act in accord

"And you were dead in your trespasses and sins in which you previously walked according to this worldly age, according to the ruler of the atmospheric domain, the spirit now working in the disobedient. We too all previously lived among them in our fleshly desires, carrying out the inclinations of our flesh and thoughts, and by nature we were children under wrath, as the others were also" (Eph. 2:1-3).

Adam and Eve

with their sinful nature. No one ever acts in a way that is contrary to his or her own inner nature apart from regeneration.

This idea is significant when reflecting upon the matters of our relationship to God. Because of the entrance of sin into the world and our inheritance of Adam's sinful nature (Rom. 5:12–19), we are by nature hostile to God and estranged from Him (Rom. 8:7; Eph. 2:13). We then have wills that do not obey God, eyes that do not see, and ears that do not hear because spiritually we are dead to God.

While we function as free moral agents with free wills, our decisions and actions are always affected by sin. In day-to-day decisions we have the ability to make free and rational choices, but these choices are always influenced by our sin nature. In regard to our relationship with God, we do not genuinely repent or turn to God without divine help because we are by nature hostile to God.

An awareness of these ideas helps to clarify frequently misunderstood concepts about the nature of sinful humanity. Our nature is depraved, but this does not mean we are as wicked as we can be. Rather the idea of depravity refers to the fact that all aspects of our being are negatively impacted by sin. Men and women still can and still do right and good things as viewed by society, but these thoughts and actions, no matter how benevolent, are sinful if not done for the glory of God. People choose to do good but not the ultimate good that is the goal of pleasing God and seeking His eternal glory. Thus depravity involves our total, willful rejection of the will and glory of God.

We are therefore totally depraved, but we cannot say that we are totally corrupt. Other factors such as environment, emotional makeup, heritage, and, of course, the continuing effect of our having been created in God's image influence the degree of corruption. The degree of wickedness, corruption, and deceitfulness differs from individual to individual and from culture to culture; but certainly some are more noble than others (Acts 17:11). Still, sin is inevitable because all in this world are estranged from God, but the biblical answer is that Jesus Christ has regained what was lost in Adam (Rom. 5:12–21). The grace of God has provided our restoration and brought about a right relationship with God, with one another, with nature, and with ourselves.

Salvation
Grace

Salvation is a *free* gift of God, and it cannot be merited by our good behavior (Rom. 3:22–24). Grace declares that salvation is not the culmination of humanity's quest for God but that it resides in the initiative of God toward men and women (Eph. 1:4–7). Even our faith is a gift of God (Eph. 2:8–9), and, as a matter of fact, all of life is such (James 1:17). If grace brings us to God, it also enables us to continue and complete our spiritual pilgrimage. This does not deny human involvement in salvation, but it does affirm the primacy of grace. When men and women receive the grace of God, it is a testimony to the impact of grace itself; but when grace is rejected, it is attributable to the hardness and sinfulness of the human heart.

Grace comes to us while we are still in our sins and brings spiritual transformation based on the accomplished cross work of Jesus Christ. Even the sanctifying work of the Spirit is enacted in those who do not merit or deserve it. In reality *grace* is *God's free and loving favor to the ill-deserving.*

> **"**
> "Let original sin make us walk with continual jealousy and watchfulness over our hearts. The sin of our nature is like a sleeping lion, the least thing that wakens it makes it rage. The sin of our nature, though it seems quiet, and lies as fire hid under the embers, yet if it be a little stirred and blown up by a temptation, how quickly may it flame forth into scandalous evils? Therefore we need to walk watchfully"—Thomas Watson.
> **"**

"As far as the east is from the west, so far has he removed our transgressions from us" (Ps. 103:12, NIV).

"He is abundantly merciful" (Eph. 2:1–10).

"For by grace you have been saved through faith; and that not of yourselves, it is the gift of God; not as a result of works, that no one should boast" (Eph. 2:8–9, NASB).

God does not graciously accept us because He sees our change for the better, as if conversion were the basis for receiving God's grace. Instead, the Bible pictures God's coming into our lives, taking us just as we are because He is abundantly merciful (Eph. 2:1–10).

Salvation is of God and is not based on the human response, yet men and women must respond to God's grace. Only persons who receive and are transformed by divine grace can make a favorable response to God's gracious invitation, but only those who do respond are indeed transformed by grace. Thus we affirm the priority of initiating grace without neglecting our responsibility to believe.

Far from violating our wills or personalities, God's grace appeals to our deepest yearnings. Therefore when we are exposed to grace, intrinsically we are drawn toward it. We therefore affirm that in response to saving grace, we are not merely passive. Neither do we want to imply that God does some and we do the rest; rather, God does all, and we do all. God does not override the will but releases the will for believing response. It is certain that convicting grace can be rejected (Matt. 23:37; Luke 7:3; Heb. 12:15); yet when we receive the gracious gift of regeneration, our wills are turned in a completely new direction. When God extends His grace to us, He is the active agent, but He always extends grace through various means. The means of grace include the preached gospel, the written Word of God, the invitation to respond to grace, the prayers of other believers, and

66

"The grace of God is love freely shown towards guilty sinners, contrary to their merit and indeed in defiance of their demerit. It is God showing goodness to persons who deserve only severity, and had no reason to expect anything but severity. We have seen why the thought of grace means so little to some church people —namely, because they do not share the beliefs about God and man which it presupposes"— J. I. Packer, *Knowing God* (Downers Grove, Ill.: InterVarsity Press, 1972), 120.

99

the faith of the respondent. This leads to the need to understand the meaning of faith.

Faith

The Bible maintains that faith is the means by which we receive and appropriate the salvation purchased for us by the cross work of our Lord Jesus Christ (Gal. 2:1–6; Eph. 2:8-9). *Faith includes a full commitment of the whole person to the Lord Jesus, a commitment that involves knowledge, trust, and obedience.* Faith is not merely an intellectual assent or an emotional response but a complete, inward spiritual change confirmed to us by the Holy Spirit. Faith is altogether brought about by God, and it is altogether the human response bringing about complete enslavement to God and full liberation from the snare of sin.

The object of faith is not the teaching about Christ but Christ himself. Though faith is more than doctrinal assent, it must include adherence to doctrine. In our belief in and commitment to Jesus Christ, we acknowledge Him as Savior from sin and Lord of our lives, even Lord of Creation (Rom. 10:9). True conversion definitely involves a belief in Christ's person as the God-Man and in His work as Savior. We must remember, however, that it is possible to have an orthodox understanding of Christ without a living faith in Him.

Conversion and Repentance

Conversion signifies our turning to Christ initiated by God. It is a great work of God's power changing the heart and infusing life into our dead spirits. It is important to recognize that the outworking of this grace in the conversion experience displays itself differently in some than in others. Not all have a "Damascus road experience" like the apostle Paul. Some are converted quietly like Lydia and others dramatically like the Philippian jailer (Acts 16). But for all it involves a turning away from sin to righteousness, and it issues in service to the world and separation without withdrawal from it.

The *turning away from sin, renouncing, and changing our minds about sin and Christ is what we mean by repentance.* It is not merely feeling sorry for ourselves but forsaking sin.

True conversion does not just stimulate our natural abilities to do better, to "turn over a new leaf"; rather it is the imparting of a new nature. Conversion must be differentiated from reformation of character; it is a radical yet progressive alteration of our very being.

Salvation Metaphors

Briefly we must mention some of the important biblical themes and metaphors or models that picture our salvation. None of these concepts completely present the full understanding of salvation.

Regeneration. This is the most frequently discussed term within popular Christianity. It is a *spiritual change by which the Holy Spirit imparts divine life.* The idea is familiar in the writings of John, Peter, and Paul and is not without Old Testament precedent. The classic presentation is found in John 3:3–8 (see also 1 Pet. 1:23; Titus 3:5–7). From John 3 comes the popular term "born again" which is better translated as "born from above" whereby God imparts righteousness to us. It is the experiential picture of our entrance into God's family, whereby adoption refers to our position in this family.

Justification is predominantly a Pauline concept, though it is found in other biblical writers, especially Luke. Justification is accomplished at the cross of Christ (Rom. 5:10), guaranteed by His Resurrection (Rom. 4:24–25), and applied to us when we believe (Rom. 5:1). While regeneration pictures an experiential imparting of righteousness, justification is a declaration of our righteousness. Experientially we still sin, but God views us as totally righteous, clothed in the robes of our Lord Jesus (Rom. 4:1–8). Because of Christ's sacrifice, God no longer counts our sins against us (2 Cor. 5:19–21). Justification is more than pardon; it is a granting of positive favor in God's sight (Rom. 3:21–26).

Adoption is primarily a Pauline picture. It carries the idea of receiving the position of full grown children of God, adopted into God's family with all the corresponding rights, privileges, and duties (Rom. 8:15, Gal. 4:1–5; Eph. 1:5, 14–15). Adoption is not entirely a past event, for the consummation of our adoption awaits the redemption of our bodies (Rom. 8:23), something hoped for as well as something already possessed.

Sanctification. Sanctification involves different aspects of our salvation and is in some sense an umbrella term. The Bible speaks of positional sanctification (1 Cor. 6:11), progressive sanctification (Rom. 6:1–4; 7:2–5), and ultimate sanctification (1 John 3:1–3). It is a work of the Father (John 17:17), the Son (Gal. 2:20), and primarily of the Spirit (2 Cor. 3:17–18). Yet it is also a work of the

"He saved us—not by works of righteousness that we had done, but according to His mercy, through the washing of regeneration and renewal by the Holy Spirit" (Tim. 3:5).

"But to all who did receive Him, He gave them the right to be children of God, to those who believe in His name" (John 1:12).

"If it is the grace of God that sets a man's feet at the entrance of the pathway of faith, it is equally the grace of God that enables him to continue and complete that pathway"—F. F. Bruce, *Commentary on the Epistle to the Hebrews* (Grand Rapids: Eerdmans, 1964), 365.

We are to strive after holiness, working out our salvation with fear and trembling.

"The sea enters into the rivers before the rivers can run into the sea. In like manner, God comes to us before we go to Him; and heaven enters into our souls before we can enter into heaven"—Peter Drelincourt.

believer (Rom. 12:1–2). The Bible does not teach a "letting go and letting God" approach to sanctification; rather, we are to strive after holiness, working out our salvation with fear and trembling. This is accomplished through the Bible's transforming effects in our lives (1 Pet. 2:2), prayer (Col. 4:2), fellowship and worship (Heb. 10:19–25), and our responses to the circumstances of life (Rom. 8:28).

Glorification. The arrival at the state of absolute righteousness is our glorification. Justification is a declaration of righteousness; sanctification is the process of becoming more righteous; and glorification is the final consummation of our righteousness (Rom. 8:28–30).

Forgiveness. The putting away of sin and its penalty is forgiveness. It includes a gracious forgetting (Eph. 4:32), a sending away of our sins (Matt. 26:28), and a putting aside or disregarding of all sin (Rom. 3:25). The Bible is the only religious book that emphasizes total and complete forgiveness (Heb. 10:17), as pictured in the account of the wayward son (Luke 15:11–32). Scripture presents the bases of forgiveness as the shedding of blood (Heb. 9:22–26), as well as our faith and repentance (Luke 17:3–10).

Union with Christ. The result of the concepts of adoption, forgive-

"Our forgiving of others will not procure forgiveness for ourselves; but our not forgiving others proves that we ourselves are not forgiven"—John Owen.

ness, and justification is pictured as the believer's new sphere of union with Christ (John 15; Rom. 6:1–11; Eph. 1:3–14). Positionally, our union with Christ presents us in a new position before God. Experientially, the union of believers with God is one of the most tender concepts expressed in Scripture; it is invisible and imperceptible to the senses; it is unfathomable, escaping all inward vision. Yet this mystery (Col. 1:27–28) cannot be dissected or denied.

Eternal Security

God is the Author and Finisher of our faith (Heb. 12:2). Salvation is from sin, for the world has primarily a need of a sin bearer (John 1:29). This involves disarming believers from the rulers and authorities of this world (Col. 2:14–15). Salvation is only in Christ (John 14:6; Acts 4:12), is imperishable (1 Pet. 1:4), and is the source of all spiritual blessing (Eph. 1:3).

"Election is the gracious purpose of God, according to which He regenerates, sanctifies, and glorifies sinners. It is consistent with the free agency of man, and comprehends all the means in connection with the end. It is a glorious display of God's sovereign goodness, and is infinitely wise, holy, and unchangeable"—*Baptist Faith and Message*, 1963.

Our salvation is secured in Christ, and nothing can separate us from the love of Christ (Rom. 8:31–39); yet our response to this truth brings our assurance. Eternal security is an objective truth, but our assurance is experiential and subjective. It is based on the work of Christ (Heb. 7:25), the witness of the Spirit (Rom. 8:14–17), and our obedience (1 John 5:11–13). God has promised to keep us from stumbling (Jude 24), having sealed us until the day of redemption (Eph. 4:30). Thus we are responsible to persevere and hold on to God. Ultimately our security in Christ comes because He has a hold on us (John 10:28–30).

Conclusion

We affirm that God has created men and women in the image of God. Humans have sinned and are alienated from God apart from saving grace. In grace, God takes the initiative in bringing sinners to Christ through the proclamation of the gospel and the human response of faith. As a result of God's grace, believers experience salvation from sin which involves conversion to God. All of salvation is of God, yet we respond in faith and commitment. The Bible expresses these truths in various metaphors, underscoring throughout that God is the Author and Finisher of our salvation.

❝

"Grace is the free sovereign favor to the ill-deserving"—B. B. Warfield, *Selected Shorter Writings* (Nutley, NJ: Presbyterian and Reformed, 1973), 2:427.

"There is nothing else that leads to the grace of God, or eternal salvation, but the word and work of God"—Martin Luther, *The Bondage of the Will* (Westwood, NJ: Revell, reprint, 1957), 139.

Further Reflection

1. What does it mean to say that humans are made in the image of God?
2. What is the relationship between divine grace and human faith in salvation?

For Additional Study

Hunt, Boyd. *Redeemed*. Nashville: Broadman & Holman, 1993.
Oden, Thomas C. *The Transforming Power of Grace*. Nashville: Abingdon, 1993.
Ryrie, Charles C. *The Grace of God*. Chicago: Moody, 1963.
Smith, David L. *With Willful Intent: A Theology of Sin*. Wheaton: BridgePoint, 1994.
Warfield, Benjamin B. *The Plan of Salvation*. Grand Rapids: Eerdmans, reprint 1975.

The Holy Spirit

Our purpose in this part of the series is to examine the primary meaning given to the Holy Spirit in the Old Testament as well as the person and work of the Holy Spirit in the New Testament, with emphasis given to the apostle Paul and the teaching regarding Christian living. The Bible reveals the Holy Spirit as the third member of the Trinity (John 14; 16; Acts 5:3–4), a distinct entity from the Father and Son.

"I will put My Spirit in you, and you will live, and I will settle you in your own land. Then you will know that I am the Lord. I have spoken, and I will do [it]." [This is] the declaration of the Lord (Ezek. 37:14).

The Spirit and the Mission of the New Church

With the coming of the Spirit at Pentecost (Acts 2), there was a universalizing of the ministry and mission of Jesus. Jesus was God's final Word to humanity, and the Spirit's role was not to give some new revelation of His own but to bear witness to Jesus and to interpret and bring out all the full implications of God's final Word. When the Spirit came in full measure at Pentecost, the church was launched. The Spirit came in order to unite believers in an unparalleled manner, creating a quality of life that had not been experienced before. The Spirit enabled believers to be far more than they were in their own natural gifts. The Spirit came as promise, not as law; as gift, not as challenge; and He came sovereignly, not conditionally.

"But the Counselor, the Holy Spirit—the Father will send Him in My name—will teach you all things and remind you of everything I have told you" (John 14:26).

The Spirit's coming brought not an emotional frenzy but a new, sovereign gift of power to the young church. Yet with the Spirit's coming was the accompanying sign of tongues of fire. Tongues were not necessary to advance the mission but to authenticate the mission's message and messengers. The tongues were given to the apostles; they were not taught. The ultimate purpose of the giving of the Spirit was for empowerment of the church's mission, which was the spreading of the good news and exalting the name of Christ.

After Pentecost, the Spirit was active primarily in (1) preaching,

No one can confess Jesus as Lord except by the Holy Spirit.

(2) teaching, (3) prophecy, (4) witnessing, (5) bringing love and guidance to the new community, and (6) the continuation of the church's mission. The Spirit was involved in the early church in Jerusalem (Acts 2–5), in the prophetic proclamation of Stephen (Acts 6–7), in the spreading of the gospel to the Gentiles (Acts 10), in the sending out of Paul and Barnabas (Acts 13), and in the establishment of the transition to the church's mature state (Acts 19).

The Spirit used various means to advance the new mission. Some of these means included trances (Acts 10), prophetic word (Acts 11), worship services (Acts 13), church councils (Acts 15), and inner constraint (Acts 16). What is obvious is that the Spirit always remained the unpredictable, mysterious, sovereign third member of the Trinity.

The Holy Spirit and Christian Life

"In Him you also, when you heard the word of truth, the gospel of your salvation—in Him when you believed—were sealed with the promised Holy Spirit. He is the down payment of our inheritance, for the redemption of the possession, to the praise of His glory" (Eph 1:13-14).

The Pauline view of the spiritual life can be summarized by the statement in 2 Corinthians 3:17b, "Where the Spirit of the Lord is, there is freedom." Paul's understanding of the Spirit must be seen from two perspectives; the Spirit in the life of the believer and the Spirit in the life of the community. We could not do justice to Paul's thought without a brief look at life in tension, including the nature of suffering in relation to life in the Spirit.

The Work of the Spirit in the Individual Believer

The apostles, especially Paul, maintained certain expectations that would accompany the coming of the age of the Spirit. The new community, characterized by enthusiasm and other manifestations of the Spirit's power, are evidence of the advent of the age to come. The active presence of the Spirit was a mark of the last days. The ministry of the Spirit authenticated the claims of Jesus as Messiah.

Paul saw the Spirit drawing attention to the glories of the risen Christ in the preaching ministry (1 Thess. 1:15; 1 Cor. 2:14). The Spirit also enabled persons to respond to the message of the glorified Christ. Indeed, it is a fundamental assumption of Paul's theology that all believers are possessors of the Spirit. In other words, no one can respond to the claims of Christ without being activated and indwelt by the Holy Spirit.

Paul told the Thessalonians that God had given them the Holy Spirit (1 Thess. 4:8). In his first letter to the Corinthians, he stated

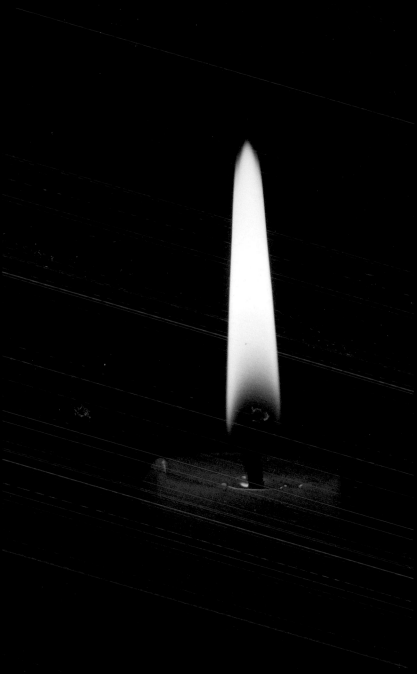

that no one can confess Jesus as Lord except by the Holy Spirit (1 Cor. 12:3). All believers have the Spirit since "if anyone does not have the Spirit of Christ, he does not belong to Christ" (Rom. 8:9). The Spirit has transformed persons from unrighteousness to those who are washed, sanctified, and justified (1 Cor. 6:10–11). In this passage, Paul draws a sharp contrast between the former life and the change the Spirit's ministry performs.

The regenerating work of the Spirit brings about new life in Christ. The new life in Christ is summarized in Paul's classic statement, "If anyone is in Christ, he is a new creation; the old has passed away, behold the new has come" (2 Cor. 5:17). The point is that the coming of the new age brought about by the Spirit creates a new person. The passing of the old does not mean the end of the old age; it continues until the return of Christ. But the old age does not remain intact; the new age has broken in. Without discussing the full ramifications of the new age, it can be said that while believers live in the old age, because they are in Christ, they belong to the new age with its new creation, and they are to live a life that is expressive of the new existence.

In addition to the Spirit's initiating and regenerating work is the Spirit's work in adoption and sanctification. Two primary passages show that the believer's conviction of being God's child is directly induced by the Holy Spirit (Rom. 8:14–17; Gal. 4:6). It is the Spirit who leads the children of God to cry out, "Abba! Father!" Adoption describes the new relationship between believers and their God.

The term *sanctification* can be used comprehensively to describe the overall process by which the new believer moves toward a life of holiness. The standard of sanctification is a holiness acceptable to God; that is, a holiness in line with the Spirit's own character (Rom. 15:16; 1 Cor. 6:11). The Spirit of God is not only active in revealing the gospel but is likewise involved in bringing the believer to further understanding (1 Cor. 2:13). This is referred to as the Spirit's work of illumination and guidance. Paul went into considerable detail in 1 Corinthians 2:10–16 in order to establish the distinction between human wisdom and the Spirit's understanding. He affirmed that without the enablement of the Spirit, a saving knowledge of God is unattainable. After receiving the gift of the Spirit, there is a capacity for understanding that was previously denied. The Spirit penetrates to the deepest understanding of God in Christ.

"We need the work of the Holy Spirit as well as the work of Christ; we need renewal of the heart as well as the atoning blood; we need to be sanctified as well as justified"—J. C. Ryle, *Holiness* (London: Clarke, 1956), 38.

The Spirit guides believers into a new way of thinking and gives them a new set of values: "Those who live according to the Spirit set their minds on the things of the Spirit" (Rom. 8:5). The mind of the Spirit is the place of reason, feeling, and will patterned after and controlled by the Holy Spirit. The renewal of the mind (Rom. 12:2), which was formerly hostile to God (Rom. 8:7), can only be achieved by and through the Spirit in opposition to carrying out the desires of the sinful flesh (Gal. 6:15; Rom. 8:4). The concept of total dependence on the empowering of the Spirit shows how utterly indispensable the Spirit is for Christian living, and it demonstrates the impossibility of any Christian not possessing the Spirit.

Paul spoke of the Spirit in contrast to the life controlled by the flesh. In Galatians 5:22–23, Paul gave his understanding of the fruit of the Spirit as "love, joy, peace, patience, kindness, goodness, faithfulness, gentleness and self-control." These virtues must be compared with the similar lists in Philippians 4:8 and Colossians 3:12–15. These Spirit-prompted virtues go beyond the cultural bounds of virtue so that, for example, believers demonstrate love by loving their enemies. The outworking of these virtues is a demonstration of the Spirit at work in the believer. The Spirit breaks the shackles of the flesh and delivers the believer from bondage to sin and the law. The bringing of liberty is one of the great outworkings of the Spirit in the new age.

"We believe in the Holy Spirit, the Lord and lifegiver, who proceeds from the Father, who is worshiped and glorified together with the Father and Son, Who spoke through the prophets"—The Constantinople Creed, 381.

"That through the Holy Spirit He [Christ] may sanctify, purify, strengthen, and comfort all who believe in Him, that He may bestow on them life and every grace and blessing"—Article III, The Augsburg Confession, 1530.

The Work of the Spirit in the New Community

Paul viewed the Holy Spirit as the basis for true unity in the body of Christ. Fellowship in the Johannine Epistles seems to be "with the Father and with his Son" (1 John 1:3). But Paul stressed "fellowship in the Spirit" (Phil. 2:1–4; 2 Cor. 13:14). The passage in Philippians enlarges on the theme of unity and suggests a mutual participation of believers through the common bond of the Spirit. It is the Spirit who binds Christians together and enables them to be of the same mind, which is the mind of Christ (Phil. 2:2–5).

The community of faith is to maintain the unity of the Spirit (1 Cor. 12; Eph. 4:16). The basis of unity is identified by Paul as the baptism in the Spirit (1 Cor. 12:13). The baptism of the Spirit is the way of initiation into the new corporate life of the community. This underscores the Spirit-dominated character of the corporate Christian life. The concept of "all given the one Spirit to drink" shows the basic solidarity of all Christians in the Spirit. It is a trans-

formation for all believers by which they are placed into the body of Christ, made possible by the Spirit. The Spirit has been given by the exalted Christ to form a new people, to join believers together in the baptism of the Spirit to constitute the body of Christ.

Similarly, the new community should be filled with the Spirit (Eph. 5:18–20). Instead of finding empowerment and illumination in wine (Eph. 5.17- 18), the church finds the basis for such in the Spirit's control and filling. The result is a worshiping community, giving thanks, singing songs of mutual edification to one another and mutually submitting one to another in the fear of Christ.

Paul gave his understanding of the fruit of the Spirit as "love, joy, peace, patience, kindness, goodness, faithfulness, gentleness and self-control."

Tension in the Spiritual Life

Life in the Spirit is to be lived out in the tension between what has been accomplished by the historical achievement of Jesus and what is yet to be fully realized in the Second Coming. The believer lives in this temporal tension. Believers live in this age, but their life pattern, their standard of conduct, their aims and goals are not those of this human-centered and prideful age. They are of the age to come. Yet the struggle with indwelling sin continues (Rom. 7:14–25), and the flesh continues to war against the Spirit (Gal. 5:16–21).

While living in the Spirit as a citizen of the new age (Phil. 3:21), believers will suffer in this age (Phil. 1:29–30). Believers live conscious of life in Adam (Rom. 5:12–21) and in Christ (Rom. 6:1–11). Such life is characterized as a tension between freedom and responsible living (Rom. 14). Yet life in the Spirit awakens the believer to the prospects of present and ultimate victories. The basis for life in the Spirit must never be forgotten. Through the death and Resurrection of Jesus Christ the Spirit applies justification, regeneration, sanctification, and ultimate glorification to the lives of believers. Life in the Spirit is living out, by the Spirit's empowerment, what believers are because of Christ.

For Paul, Christianity was essentially spiritual. That is, Christianity is interpreted through the category of the Spirit. This makes it inevitable that Paul should also give greater significance to the ethical aspect of the spiritual life. The Spirit enables the believer to obey in the midst of struggling and suffering.

The most genuine utterance of the Spirit in the assembly of believers is not ecstatic speech but prophecy, since the intention and criterion of the worship service was that God should become manifest for the people (1 Cor. 14:23–25). Individual believers experience the Spirit primarily in prayer when they call upon God as Abba! Father! (Gal. 4:6; Rom. 8:15). The Spirit provides divine enablement to the believer struggling in prayer (Rom. 8:26–27). The immediacy of devotion to God does not come forth from innate human capacity but from the Spirit. In prayer the Spirit gives a deep awareness that one has been accepted through the love of God. When the Spirit reaches to God's children, the love of God reaches out (Rom. 5:5).

The Spirit is ultimately made known as the power that generates openness before God, enablement in struggle, and openness in prayer. The Spirit is the down payment of future glory (Eph. 1:13;

> **"**
> "We cannot rightly attribute to the Spirit any teaching which does not shed light on Jesus, or any religious experience which is not congruous with the life of Jesus"—Michael Green, *I Believe in the Holy Spirit* (Grand Rapids: Eerdmans, 1983), 52.
> **"**

For Paul, Christianity was essentially spiritual. That is, Christianity is interpreted through the category of the Spirit.

4:30) that will be inherited at the Second Coming. Until then the community experiences life in the Spirit in such a way that can be characterized as liberty. In the spiritual life liberty comes through obedience, and glory comes through suffering.

Conclusion

We have seen that almost every aspect of the Christian experience is influenced by the Spirit's actions. The Spirit was dominantly viewed as the source of empowerment in the Old Testament. After the Ascension of Jesus, the Spirit came at Pentecost in His fullness to universalize the ministry of Christ while exalting Him in the expansion of the church's new mission. It was observed that the Spirit characterizes the life of the individual believer as well as the life of the new community of faith. Life in the Spirit brings freedom to believers, a freedom from sin and law and toward obedience that must be exercised in responsible living.

"What then? Is the Spirit God? Most certainly. Well then is He consubstantial? Yes, if He is God"—Gregory of Nazianzus, *Orations* 31.10.

Consubstantial

Consubstantial means "of the same substance." Father, Son, and Holy Spirit are three persons but one substance. Each person of the Trinity is God.

Further Reflection

1. How does the Holy Spirit's work affect our spiritual development?
2. What are the practical implications of the Spirit's being present not only in individuals but also in the community of faith?

For Additional Study

Bruner, Frederick Dale. *A Theology of the Holy Spirit*. Grand Rapids: Eerdmans, 1970.

Green, Michael. *I Believe in the Holy Spirit*. Grand Rapids: Eerdmans, 1975.

Packer, J. I. *Keep in Step with the Spirit*. Old Tappan, N. J.: Revell, 1984.

The Church

The church is the community of men and women who have responded to God's offer of salvation. It provides order, organization, and mission directives for the people of God. As far as humanly possible, all believers in the Lord involve themselves in the visible, organized church of Jesus Christ, and every person in the church should be rightly related to Jesus Christ by faith. The people of God on earth at any one time plus all believers in heaven and earth make up the true, invisible, universal church. We will examine the nature and mission of the church, including the order and organization of the church, its worship, mission, ministry, fellowship, ordinances, and discipline.

"Now if you will listen to Me and carefully keep My covenant, you will be My own possession out of all the peoples, although all the earth is Mine, and you will be My kingdom of priests and My holy nation. These are the words that you are to say to the Israelites" (Exod. 19:5-6).

The Nature of the Church
The Inauguration of the Church
The word *church* can be used in a variety of ways. It can be used

"You yourselves, as living stones, are being built into a spiritual house for a holy priesthood to offer spiritual sacrifices acceptable to God through Jesus Christ" (1 Pet. 2:5).

to talk about a place where believers gather, a local organization of believers, a universal body of believers, a particular denomination (like the Presbyterian Church), or an organization of believers related to a particular area or nation (like the Church of Scotland).

The biblical idea of church must be understood from the usage of *ekklesia* (the Greek word for *church*) in the New Testament. The basic idea means "a gathered group of people." In the Bible *ekklesia* has a variety of meanings, but most references point to a local body of believers. The term occurs 114 times in the New Testament, of which 109 refer to the local or universal church of Jesus Christ. In Acts 19:32, 41, there is reference to an unruly mob, and in Acts 19:39, the term is translated as a lawful assembly. First Thessalonians 1:1 points to a specific church, while Galatians 1:22 refers to a group of churches. Ephesians 1:22–23 and Colossians 1:18 look beyond the local churches to the spiritual unity of the universal church. We can see that there are several usages of the word *church* in the New Testament.

"On this rock I will build My church, and the gates of Hades will not overpower it" (Matt. 16:18).

The church was inaugurated at Pentecost (Acts 2) as God's new society (Eph. 2:15). It was founded upon the finished work of Christ (John 19:30) and the baptizing work of the Spirit (1 Cor. 12:13). The church was a mystery (Eph. 3:9–11), was prophesied by Christ (Matt. 16:18), and was revealed at the Spirit's coming at Pentecost. The church was built upon the foundation of Christ's apostles, with Christ Jesus Himself the Cornerstone (Eph. 2:20–21).

Characteristics of the Church

What the believing community is precedes an understanding of what the church *does*. The church is both in origin and in end God's church. We do not create the church by our efforts but receive it as a gift of God. It is constituted by Him and for Him. Membership is by divine fellowship of those who have trusted in Christ and are indwelt by the Holy Spirit, a community of believers who have been called as saints.

The New Testament presents several models or images of the church, reflecting more of a Judaistic than of a Hellenistic background. The church was presented through pictures and images rather than logical proposition. Some of these images include the church as the fellowship of the Spirit (Phil. 2:2), the household of God (Gal. 6:10), the new creation (Eph. 2:15), the body of Christ (Eph. 1:22), the temple of the Holy Spirit (Eph. 2:21), the pillar of

"How much more clearly could the biblical writer put the fact that there is only one people of God even though there are at least two aspects: Israel and the church. God's olive tree began with the roots God planted in the promises given to the patriarchs. From this root grew the Jewish people. . . . The doctrine of the church must carefully set forth the unity and singularity of the people of God, but it must also be careful to note that the gifts and calling of God are irrevocable"— Walter C. Kaiser, Jr.

The church was inaugurated at Pentecost (Acts 2) as God's new society (Eph. 2:15). It was founded upon the finished work of Christ (John 19:30)

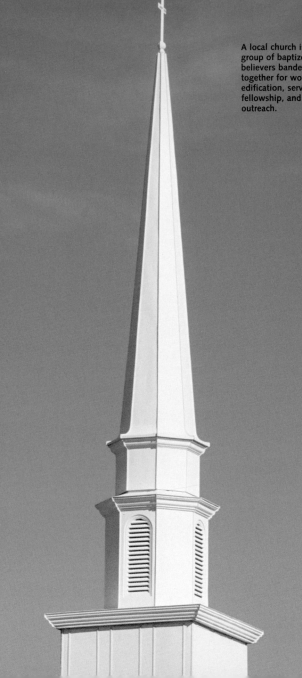

A local church is a group of baptized believers banded together for worship, edification, service, fellowship, and outreach.

the truth (1 Tim. 3:15), and the bride of Christ (Rev. 19:7).

The church is multisided, as these images demonstrate. The idea of the church as the people of God pictures its universality; that is, believers who cross all segments of society are in touch with one another (Gal. 3:28). The image of the new creation pictures Christ's victory over evil as a new humanity in the midst of the old. The household of God points to the visible form of God's people who relate to one another in community and constitute the new creation. The body of Christ shows the presence of Christ in the world, though it is mystically experienced and known. The church is more than a human organization but is a visible and tangible expression of the people who are related to Christ.

Joining with the church throughout the ages, we maintain that the church is *one, holy, universal*, and *apostolic*. The church's oneness includes unity one with another, visible and invisible (John 17:1–26; 1 Cor. 12:4–6; Eph. 4:16). The completed holiness of the church will be completed in Christ. It reminds the church it is to be visibly holy in spite of its present sinfulness, thus the need to be tolerant with one another's weaknesses (1 Pet. 1:15–16). Confessing the church as universal points to the need to be inclusive of all branches of the true church rather than to maintain an exclusivistic view that one branch contains the whole truth (John 16:13; 1 Tim. 3:15). Also it says that the church's mission is to all nations (Matt. 28:19–20). Apostolicity calls the church to remain faithful to the normative nature of apostolic doctrine and practice (Matt. 16:16–18; Eph. 2:20; Jude 3).

To this point our discussion has focused on general truths about the universal church, the community of believers of all time in heaven and on all parts of the earth. Our focus in the remainder of this section will concentrate primarily on the nature and ministry of the local church, which is a specific group of God's people in a specific place. More definitely we can say that a local church is a group of baptized believers banded together for worship, edification, service, fellowship, and outreach; accepting spiritual leadership; willing to minister to all segments of society through the various gifts in the body; and regularly practicing ordinances.

Order and Organization of the Church

The church is to do everything decently and in order (1 Cor. 14:40). For the church to function in this way, there is a need for leadership

"We believe that this true Church must be governed by the spiritual policy which our Lord has taught us in his Word"— Article XXX, The Belgic Confession, 1561.

(Acts 14:23; Titus 1:5; Heb. 13:17). The leadership of the church includes two offices: overseers (referred to as pastors, elders, or bishops in the New Testament: Acts 20:17, 28; 1 Tim. 3:1, Titus 1:5; James 5:14; and 1 Pet. 5:23) and deacons (Phil. 1:1; 1 Tim. 3:8).

The first group of leaders is responsible for general oversight, administration, teaching, and shepherding. The second group of leaders has the responsibilities of service, helping, family care, and visitation. The distinction in function can be determined from the differences in the purposes and qualifications listed in Scripture. Generally speaking, the overseers are responsible for teaching and administration while the deacons are responsible for care and service.

The qualifications of leadership are listed in 1 Timothy 3 and Titus 1. The great degree of detail in the lists should point to the high demands to be placed upon the church's leaders. If persons desire the office of overseer, it is a fine work they desire to do (1 Tim. 3:1). The primary qualification is that overseers should be "blameless" or "above reproach." The lists from the two passages include twenty character qualities and one requirement concerning ability ("able to teach"). This should say much to the contemporary emphasis upon personality and ability and the little concern given to spirituality and character in many congregations. The standards in today's churches are often backwards from the guidelines presented in Scripture.

The list for deacons (1 Tim. 3:8–13) is similar, though it does not contain the same detail. Two obvious differences are present. The first is that the deacons are not required to be able to teach. This does not mean that deacons are unable to teach or should not teach but merely that it is not a requirement for the functions of the diaconal office. The second is that deacons should not be double-tongued. This seemingly implies that deacons are responsible for the offering; visitation and counseling; care of the sick, the poor, and the needy; and the distribution of the Lord's Supper. This type of ministry demands personal involvement, and deacons will have access to information about the private lives of the church members. Thus deacons must not be gossips or those who distort the truth.

Additional order and organization in the church develops from needs among the congregation and the spiritual gifts available for ministry in particular settings (1 Cor. 12; Eph. 4:11–16). The function of the church is more important than its form as the entire congregation submits to Jesus Christ as Lord and head of the church

"The Lord Jesus is the Head of the Church, which is composed of all His true disciples, and in Him is invested supremely all power for its government. According to His commandment, Christians are to associate themselves into particular societies or churches; and to each of these churches He hath given needful authority for administering that order, discipline and worship which He hath appointed. The regular officers of a Church are Bishops or Elders, and Deacons"—Article XIV, The Abstract of Principles, 1859.

Worship is central in the existence and continuation of the church as presented in the New Testament.

(Eph. 1); so that there is no authoritarian leadership (1 Pet. 5:13) in the local congregation. Instead, there is mutual participation, admonition, and encouragement (Rom. 1:12; Heb. 10:24–25), as well as mutual submission one to another (Eph. 5:21).

The Mission of the Church
The Church in Praise and Worship

Worship is central in the existence and continuation of the church as presented in the New Testament. The ultimate purpose of the church is the worship and praise of the One who called it into being (Eph. 1:4–6). To worship God is to ascribe to Him the supreme worth which He alone is worthy to receive. Worship is desired by God (John 4:24) and is made possible by His grace. To worship God includes reverence and adoration (Rev. 4:11). It also involves the expression of awe, as well as the Spirit-enabled service expressed in prayer (Acts 13:2–3), giving (Rom. 15:27), or the ministry of the gospel (Rom. 15:16). Worship in the community produces a total ministry of life that is pleasing to God (Rom. 12:1–2). There is, thus, a close relationship between worship and a life of service to God.

The elements of Christian worship are similar to those found in

> 66
>
> "Forms of worship should provide two things: channels for the mind to apprehend the truth of God's reality, and channels for the heart to respond to the beauty of that truth—that is, forms to ignite the affections with biblical truth, and forms to express the affections with biblical passion"—John Piper, *Desiring God*, Portland: Multnomah Books, 1986), 92.
>
> 99

the Old Testament, yet there are two new factors at the very heart of the New Testament that bring about a decisive reorientation. The first of these is that Christian worship is in its very core and essence the worship of God the Father through the Son. The Christological orientation is new although the essential elements remain. The worshiping community stands in a personal relation to God on the basis of adoption in Christ. Prayer is made in the name of the Son (John 16:23). The works of God in the Son are the theme of this praise (Eph. 1:2). The confession is the confession of Jesus as Lord (Rom. 10:9; 1 Cor. 12:3). Preaching is setting forth the work of Christ (2 Cor. 4:5), and the Lord's Supper is the celebration of the new and final exodus, the showing forth of Christ's sacrifice for sin (1 Cor. 11:26). Giving is on the basis of God's gift in His Son (2 Cor. 9:15). The focus of the church's worship upon the exalted Christ gives a new depth and content to the worshiping community.

The first new aspect is grounded in the person and work of Christ, while the second new aspect of the church's worship is influenced by the Holy Spirit. The church's worship of God the Father is through the Son, in and by God the Holy Spirit. Prayer comes with the divine aid of the Spirit (Rom. 8:26). Praise is rejoicing in the Spirit (Eph. 5:18–20). Confession of sins is under the conviction of the Holy Spirit (1 Cor. 12:3). Holy Scripture is inspired by the Holy Spirit and illumined by the Spirit as well (2 Tim. 3:16; 1 Cor. 2:14). Preaching is in the power of the Holy Spirit (1 Cor. 2:4), and the Lord's Supper is in the fellowship of the Spirit (Acts 2). Liberty flows from love, which is a fruit of the Holy Spirit (Gal. 5:22), and a life of worship flows from walking in the Spirit (Gal. 5:16). Fitting and acceptable worship can only be offered by and through the Holy Spirit.

The Church in Ministry

"They have no share in this Spirit who do not join in the activity of the church. . . . For where the church is, there is the Spirit of God; and where the Spirit is there is the church and every kind of grace"—Irenaeus, *Against Heresies*, III.24.I.

Every member of the local church is a believer-priest before God and for one another. Jesus Christ is the Head of the church as well as its High Priest (Heb. 3:1). Each member functions as a priest who worships, offers praise and thanksgiving (Heb. 13:15–16), and offers himself or herself as a sacrifice for ministry (Rom. 12:1). Each believer is to function in his or her office of priest within the church. To enable us to do so, the Spirit of God has equipped believers with spiritual gifts for the purpose of ministry. Spiritual gifts are God-given abilities for service (Rom. 12; 1 Cor. 12; Eph. 4).

Paul gave lists of the gifts but proceeded to the more excellent way of Christian love (1 Cor. 12:31). Paul did not deny that spectacular gifts have a place, but he insisted that the important thing is the manifestation of ethical qualities, especially love, which the presence of the Spirit in the heart of the believers makes possible. The apostle assumed that all believers share in the gifts of the Spirit and that all are for the common good (1 Cor. 12:4–7). It is the concept of the edification of the body of Christ (1 Cor. 14:1–3) that is primary in understanding Paul's view of the place of gifts in the churches. Gifts are for the empowerment of believers so that the primary ministries of the believing community can be effectively accomplished. These ministries include evangelism (Matt. 28:19–20), edification and teaching (Eph. 4:11–16), and social service (James 1:27).

The Church in Fellowship

The church is a community of men and women who relate to one another because of their relationship to Jesus Christ (Acts 2.44–45; 1 John 1.3; 3:11–18). When genuine fellowship takes place, communication is encouraged, authenticity is increased, intimacy is developed, freedom of expression is encouraged, mutual burden bearing is primary, and prayer becomes specific, creating a sense of belonging. Belonging creates identity, bringing about the spiritual community among the family of God.

The Ordinances of the Church

The ordinances of the church are two, baptism and the Lord's Supper. Both have been commanded by our Lord to be continued as symbols of the Lord's ongoing presence in His church.

Baptism. Christian baptism has its background in the Old Testament act of ritual purification, proselyte baptism, and the baptism of John. Jesus began His public ministry by association with John's baptism, probably not as a sign of repentance but as the King of the kingdom (Matt. 3:13–17; John 1:19–34). According to John 4.2, Jesus Himself probably did not baptize. Jesus was baptized to identify with sinners in order to fulfill all righteousness. The church is commanded to continue the practice of Christian baptism as an aspect of discipling the nations (Matt. 28:19–20).

In the early chapters of Acts, beginning with Pentecost, baptism is closely associated with repentance as a qualification for member-

> " It is those who know Him who bring Him to others. That is why the Church, the whole body of Christians showing Him to one another, is so important"—C. S. Lewis, *Mere Christianity* (New York: Macmillan, 1952) 163.

"

ship in the Christian community (Acts 2:37–41). The references to baptism "in the name of Jesus" are probably attempts to distinguish Christian baptism from Jewish proselyte baptism rather than a specific baptismal formula (Acts 2:38; 8:16).

For Paul baptism was primarily an act of identification with the death, burial, and Resurrection of Christ. Also it serves as a sign of covenant relationship with Christ and His people (Rom. 6:1–4; Col. 2:9–13). Paul did not conceive of baptism as an essential saving ordinance or sacrament as is clearly indicated in 1 Corinthians 1:10–18. For the worshiping community baptism is the initiation act whereby one is made a member of the community, the body of Christ, identifying with Christ and His people. The act of baptism is not restricted to any class of people (Gal. 3:27–28). There is no distinction of race (Jew or Greek), gender (male or female), or social status (slave or free). All are regarded as having been baptized into Christ as a result of having put on Christ (Eph. 4:2–6; Col. 3:10).

Baptism is essentially connected with death and resurrection and not with cleansing. Baptism signifies burial with Christ in His death, but baptism also means new life, sharing with Christ's risen life. It exhibits the transition that has occurred, having moved from death to life. This involves the believer in the actual dying and rising of Christ in a kind of reenactment. Also it shows that death has taken

Lord's Supper relief

River Jordan, where Jesus was baptized

place in the life of the believer and a new life has begun. The new life in the community of faith requires a whole new set of values. The act of baptism is a valuable teaching medium for new believers and the entire church in order for the symbolic meaning of baptism to be communicated.

Lord's Supper. When the church celebrates the Supper, it does so to remember Jesus' broken body and shed blood and the love that motivated His bearing the cross. The cross is preached, but it is also shown in the bread and the cup. The Christian community follows the dynamic example of the Passover. The elements of the Supper takes believers back to the scenes of redemption, not in a nostalgic reflection, but as a vivid reminder of the One whose they are now and who is coming again. The celebration of the Supper is central to the church's worship and thus should be a regular and frequent occurrence (Acts 20:7; 1 Cor. 11:24). Only believers who are a part of the body of Christ are entitled to partake of it.

"He has left us this dark glass, wherein we may see His face till He return with a full glory; and is it an affection to Him never to look upon His picture, the medal of Himself, wherein He has engraven love; all that He did, all that He purchased, all His fullness, all His treasures . . . ? Well, but we may remember Christ other ways without this ceremony. We may, but do we?"
—Stephen Charnock.

85

The Discipline of the Church

Perhaps the most neglected practice in the contemporary Christian community is the discipline of the church. Discipline rests upon the fact that God Himself disciplines His children (Heb. 12:6). God disciplines His own, but He has ordained mediate discipline by the church concerning those affairs that concern the life and walk of the local body. Discipline is based on the holiness of God (Heb. 12:11), the command of Christ (Matt. 18:18), and the practice of the apostles (1 Cor. 5).

"The nature and end of judgment or sentence must be corrective, not vindictive; for healing, not destruction"—John Owen.

The practice of discipline must be done with great care. We should remember that the apostle Paul had much to say about the sins at Corinth, yet He singled out only one sin among the community for discipline in 1 Corinthians 5. The categories for discipline in the New Testament are many (Matt. 18:15–17; Rom. 16:17–18; 2 Thess. 3:14–15; 1 Tim. 1:20). Often public rebuke is called for at these times (Matt. 18:17; Rom. 16:17; 1 Cor. 5:4–5; 1 Tim. 1:20).

The forms of discipline include warning and admonition (1 Thess. 5:12–14), withholding of fellowship (2 Thess. 3:6, 17), abstaining from association (1 Cor. 5:11–15), and excommunication (1 Tim. 1:20). The act of discipline is to be performed in love and humility. The purpose of all discipline must be to win back the erring (2 Cor. 2:4; Gal. 6:1). The ultimate goal is restoration to fellowship, but the immediate goal must be shame (2 Thess. 3:14) and sorrow (2 Cor. 2:7). Yet there is warning against excessive punishment that produces excessive sorrow (2 Cor. 2:7), though there is need for godly sorrow that brings about repentance (2 Cor. 7:10). Discipline protects the church from further decay (1 Cor. 5:6). Finally, it serves as a reminder of the propensity toward sin on behalf of all (2 Cor. 7:11).

Conclusion

God called the church into being for fellowship with Himself and with other believers. The church has a dual purpose in the world; it is to be a holy priesthood (1 Pet. 2:5) and to declare the wonderful deeds of God, who called the believing community out of darkness into His marvelous light (1 Pet. 2:9). We confess the church as one, holy, universal, and apostolic and believe that God intends for all believers to be involved in local churches, worshiping, ministering, serving, fellowshipping, and celebrating together. In addition to these functions, the church has a missionary task that is not optional and is for the world, not merely for itself.

Further Reflection

1. How can the New Testament emphasis upon the corporate and covenant people be emphasized properly in our individualistic culture?
2. How can churches balance concerns for worship, fellowship, edification, and outreach ministry?

For Additional Study

Basden, Paul and David S. Dockery, eds. *The People of God*. Nashville: Broadman & Holman, 1991.

Carson, Donald A., ed. *The Church in the Bible and the World*. Grand Rapids: Baker, 1987.

Martin, Ralph P. *The Worship of God*. Grand Rapids: Eerdmans, 1985.

Saucy, Robert. *The Church in God's Program*. Chicago: Moody, 1972.

Snyder, Howard A. *The Community of the King*. Downers Grove: InterVarsity, 1977.

Last Things

Individual eschatology examines the phenomenon of death as an individual experience and the question of the intermediate state, which is the state of the dead in the period between death and the final resurrection.

We must be more cautious in our interpretation of the Bible's reference to future matters. Our confidence in the trustworthiness of the Bible is the same, though our confidence and certainty in our interpretation of such matters is more guarded. Whether concerning the Second Coming, death, the resurrection or judgment, teaching on these matters in the New Testament is presented as an incentive for obedient and holy living.

Death

No escape avails. Sooner or later, unless the Lord Jesus Christ should return, we will all die (Heb. 9:26–28). Physical death is variously represented in Scripture. It is spoken of as the death of the body, as distinguished from the soul (Matt. 10:28) or as the separation of body and soul. Never is it spoken of as annihilation but rather as the termination of physical life. According to Scripture, however, death is not merely a biological phenomenon but is a consequence of disobedience to the command of God (Gen. 2:16–17; Prov. 8:35–36).

Instead of being something natural, it is an expression of divine anger, a judgment on sin (Rom. 6:23). Adam's sin brought death not only upon himself but also upon his descendants (Rom. 5:12–21). Since death is a punishment for sin and believers are redeemed from sin and its guilt and penalty, we must ask why Christians still die. It is clear that death cannot be a punishment for them but must be considered as an aspect of the sanctification process leading to ultimate glorification. It is the consummation of believers' dying unto sin. Death's

ultimate defeat has been manifested in the Resurrection of Jesus Christ (1 Cor. 15:54–57).

Sooner or later we will all die.

The Intermediate State

The idea of the intermediate state refers to the state of the dead during the period after death and prior to the final resurrection. The soul/spirit, the immaterial aspect of believers, will at death be made perfect in holiness and pass immediately into glory (2 Cor. 5:6–8; Phil. 1:21–24). The body, the material portion, remains in the grave after death until the final resurrection (1 Thess. 4:14). At death the soul consciously rests in the presence of God (Luke 16:22–23) or in torment until the body is raised. Then the whole person exists eternally in a condition established by God's just and righteous judgment. Those who suffer are punished to the degree of divine truth that they refused (see Matt. 11:21–22). Those glorified with Christ receive His inheritance as a gift and will dwell in the new heavens and new earth (Rev. 21–22).

"And if I go and prepare a place for you, I will come back and take you to be with me that you also may be where I am" (John 14:3, NIV).

The Resurrection

Scripture teaches that at the return of Christ the dead will be raised up (Dan. 12:2; John 11:24–25; 1 Cor. 15). The resurrection will be a bodily resurrection similar to the resurrection of Christ. The redemption of the body will occur at this time (Rom. 8:23; 1 Cor. 15). Both the righteous and the wicked will be raised (various millennial viewpoints see the chronology of the resurrection(s) differently). For the wicked, the reunion of body and soul will issue in the penalty of eternal death and for the righteous an act of deliverance and glorification forever.

The Return of Christ

Throughout the history of humankind, people have sought, worked, and died attempting to bring about peace and justice on the earth. It is the responsibility of the church to work for and pray for peace and justice on earth, but ultimate peace and justice are precluded by the sinfulness of humanity. Only when God's rule and reign come to full manifestation will history know true peace. Corporate eschatology deals with those events that will occur at the close of human history. Included in this discussion will be the topics of the Second Coming of Christ, the millennium, the general resurrection, the final judgment, and eternal state. It is to the return of Christ that the church has expectantly looked since the Lord's Ascension (Acts 1:9–11).

Christ came first in the form of a servant. He will return as the Judge of all humankind (1 Thess. 5:1–3; John 5:24–27). At the first coming He inaugurated His kingdom; at His Second Coming He will consummate His kingdom. The Second Coming will be physical and personal, as were His Resurrection and Ascension (Acts 1:10–11).

The coming of Christ will be immediately preceded by a cosmic and terrestrial distress (Luke 21:25–27). Christ's return will bring a judgment upon the world that is sudden, unexpected, and inescapable (Matt. 24:42–44). The Antichrist figure is to arise prior to the Second Coming. He will be decisively overthrown (2 Thess. 2:18).

"And just as it is appointed for people to die once—and after this, judgment—so also the Messiah, having been offered once to bear the sins of many, will appear a second time, not to bear sin, but to bring salvation to those who are waiting for Him" (Heb. 9:27-28).

The kingdom of God, God's rule and reign, will be consummated and fully established at the return of Christ. In some sense Christ's redemptive kingdom is already realized in His church through the hearts and lives of believers (Rom. 14:17; Col. 1:13). There is also a future sense of Christ's kingdom that is not yet realized throughout the earth and awaits the fullness of His kingship (Isa. 11:9; Rom. 8:18–27; Rev. 20:1–6). The fullness of the kingdom, the future rule of Christ, is not identical with the final, eternal state after the establishment of the new creation, the new heavens, and the new earth (Isa. 65; Rev. 21). We can affirm that while the ultimate

Christianization of the world will never occur, there will be a great outpouring of God's grace in the end times as the gospel is proclaimed throughout the world (Matt. 24:3–31; Rom. 11:35–36). These grand truths have been systematized in four major ways referred to as postmillennialism, amillennialism, dispensational premillennialism, and historical premillennialism.

The Millennium

The term *millennium* is derived from the reference to the thousand-year reign of Christ with the saints in Revelation 20:4–6. The various millennial views reflect different understandings of the nature of this period and different interpretations of the chronological relationship of the Second Coming of Christ to the millennial period and other events of the last days.

Postmillennialism. According to this view, Christ will return after (post) a long period of expansion and spiritual prosperity for the church, brought about by the preaching of the gospel; the Spirit's blessing; and the church's work toward righteousness, justice, and peace. The period is not a literal thousand years, but this extended time of spiritual prosperity in this system includes:

The Resurrection is the core of the Christian message.

"But when the Antichrist shall have devastated all things in this world . . . then the Lord will come from heaven in the clouds, in the glory of the Father, sending this man and those who followed him into the lake of fire; but bringing in for the righteous the times of the Kingdom" —Irenaeus, *Against Heresies*, 5:35:2.

1. The kingdom of God is primarily a present reality.
2. A conversion of all nations will take place prior to Christ's return.
3. A long period of earthly peace will occur.
4. The kingdom expands gradually through the proclamation of the gospel, bringing about a kingdom of peace and light.
5. The kingdom is primarily understood in qualitative, not quantitative, terms.
6. At the end of the kingdom, there will be a time of spiritual falling away.
7. The kingdom will end with the personal, bodily return of Jesus.
8. The Lord's return will be followed immediately by the resurrection of all the righteous and unrighteous and the judgment of all.
9. What is true of the gospel's spread from individual to individual is likewise true of its spread through society's institutions and activities, physical environment, houses, education, politics, and both national and international affairs. In this way the whole mass of humanity will be imbued with and governed by Christian principles and support.

Amillennialism. Amillennialists believe there will be no (the negative "a") literal thousand-year reign of Christ with the saints on earth. The return of Christ is followed by the general resurrection of both the righteous and the wicked, the last judgment, and the passage into the eternal state. Some specific beliefs include:

1. The two resurrections in Revelation 20:4–5 are interpreted whereby the first is spiritual and the second is physical.
2. The thousand years in Revelation 20 is symbolic.
3. The book of Revelation is understood in a cyclical fashion.
4. Revelation 20 must be understood historically in relation to the rest of the book.
5. There is no expectation of revealed prophecy to be fulfilled in the future, except for the general beliefs about the Lord's return. Basically this viewpoint holds that all has been fulfilled in Christ or will be fulfilled in the new earth.
6. Generally there is a lack of prophetic interest in contrast to premillennialism.
7. There is a sense of imminency that is shared by premillennialists.
8. Like premillennialism and contrary to postmilllennialism, there

is a general view that things will get worse before Christ's triumph in the end times.

Dispensational Premillennialism. This system teaches that Christ will return prior (*pre*) to the millennium, understood as a literal thousand-year period, and prior to the seven-year period, known as the great tribulation (Dan. 9:27; Rev. 7:14; 11:2). Christ will come secretly for the church and then publicly with His church to institute the millennial kingdom. The church does not go through the tribulation period. More specifically, some primary beliefs include:

"The Spirit of the LORD will rest on Him— a Spirit of wisdom and understanding, a Spirit of counsel and strength, a Spirit of knowledge and of the fear of the LORD.... But He will judge the poor righteously and execute justice for the oppressed of the land. He will strike the land with discipline from His mouth, and He will kill the wicked with a command from His lips... The wolf will live with the lamb, and the leopard will lie down with the goat. The calf, the young lion, and the fatling will be together, and a child will lead them" (Isa. 11:2,4,6). .

1. The Bible is to be interpreted literally, including the passage in Revelation 20.
2. There is a difference between Israel and the church in the plan of God.
3. The promises and covenants given to Israel will find their ultimate fulfillment in ethnic Israel.
4. Jesus came to offer the kingdom to Israel, but it was rejected.
5. The church is a parenthesis between this rejection and the millennium.
6. The church will not go through the tribulation. The saints in Matthew 24 who are pictured in the tribulation refer to ethnic Israel.
7 The coming of Christ has two aspects:
    (1) the rapture of the church as the first aspect when Christ appears in the clouds and
    (2) the Second Coming of Christ when He comes with the church to the earth.

Historical Premillennialism. This position teaches that Christ will return prior (pre) to the millennium, which may or may not be understood as a literal thousand-year reign of Christ; but it is after the great tribulation (posttribulation). Historical premillennialists believe that the church will go through the tribulation period. Some of their beliefs include:

"Men of Galilee, why do you stand looking up into heaven? This Jesus, who has been taken from you into heaven, will come in the same way that you have seen Him going into heaven" (Acts 1:11).

1. Christ will come back to earth to reign over His kingdom, which will be an earthly one.
2. The two resurrections of Revelation 20 are both physical (contrary to amillennialists' view).

3. Christ will reign with righteousness and justice over His subjects.

4. The standard of life in the Sermon on the Mount, while applicable teaching for the church today, will become a reality in the kingdom.

5. The return of the Lord will be a unitary event (not two stages as in dispensationalism).

6. The thousand-year reign of Revelation 20 is understood as a qualitative period without specifics regarding its length.

7. The church will go through the tribulation, and then Christ will return.

8. Imminency refers to an impending coming rather than an any-moment coming.

9. The church's hope is not for deliverance from the tribulation but in the Lord's coming.

10. The church has in some sense replaced national Israel (though there is still a future for Israel) as God's covenant people.

11. The kingdom is present and future and is primarily understood as the rule and reign of God rather than the realm of God.

All positions agree that Christ will come again physically and visibly, and the church's hope is focused in Him. When He returns, He will consummate God's kingdom. The rule and reign of God will be completely expressed as God's victory over sin, evil, Satan, and death is accomplished.

The Last Judgment

The teaching of the resurrection leads to the throne of final judgment (again the chronology and types of judgments differ according to millennial views). In the first coming of Christ, He came as Savior; in His Second Coming He will return as Judge of all humankind (John 12:47–48; Acts 17:31). God's judgment will come according to the standard revealed in God's Word and will vary based upon the revelation available to different groups of people (Matt. 11:20–24). Those who have not heard the gospel, the heathen, will be judged by the law of nature and conscience (Rom. 2:12); Jews, by the Old Testament (Rom. 2:17–28). Those who have heard the full gospel revelation will be judged by it (Rom. 3:19–20). God will give every person his or her due. Every individual of the human race will have to appear before the judgment seat (Matt. 25:32; Rev. 20:12). Satan

"For God will bring every act to judgment, including every hidden thing, whether good or evil" (Eccl. 12:14).

and demons will be judged (Matt. 25:41; Jude 6), and believers will appear before the judgment seat of Christ to be judged for their works (2 Cor. 5:10).

The Eternal State

The last judgment determines the final state of those who appear before the judgment seat. Their final state is either one of everlasting misery and separation from God or one of eternal blessedness. In the final state the wicked are consigned to the place of condemnation called hell, an eternal lake of fire (Rev. 20:14–15). They will for all eternity be deprived of divine favor and will suffer punishment for sins. The final state of believers will be preceded by the judgment of the present world and the establishment of a new creation. The abode of the righteous will be heaven, a place prepared by Christ (John 14:2). Heaven is not merely spiritual but is the establishment of the new heavens and new earth (Rev. 21–22). In the eternal state, creation itself will be freed from the effects of sin and the curse upon the earth (Gen. 3). This fullness of life is enjoyed in communion with God, which is really the essence of eternal life (Rev. 21:3). All will enjoy perfect bliss, but apparently there will be degrees in the enjoyments of heaven (Dan. 12:3).

Heaven is not merely spiritual but is the establishment of the new heavens and new earth (Rev. 21–22).

Conclusion

God's final rule and reign bring victory when Christ returns to establish and consummate His kingdom. Regardless of the positive and industrious attempts by men and women to bring about righteousness and peace to earth, true peace and righteousness will occur only when Christ returns. The agelong quest of the nations can only be fulfilled by the work of Christ. We have seen that sincere believers differ over their understanding of the nature and chronology of Christ's return as well as the kingdom itself. But all agree that following His return, the dead will be raised, both the righteous and the wicked. This leads to judgment and then to the eternal state: condemnation for the wicked and eternal bliss for believers as God's eternal glory is manifested in His victorious rule and reign.

Further Reflection

1. How do the scriptural truths about God's rule and reign impact your spiritual life?
2. How do these truths impact the mission of the church?

For Additional Study

Clouse, Robert G., ed. *The Meaning of the Millennium*. Downers Grove: InterVarsity, 1977.

Dockery, David S. *Our Christian Hope*. Nashville: LifeWay Press, 1998.

Hoekema, Anthony. *The Bible and the Future*. Grand Rapids: Eerdmans, 1979.

Ladd, George E. *The Blessed Hope*. Grand Rapids: Eerdmans, 1962.

Smith, Wilbur. *The Biblical Doctrine of Heaven*. Chicago: Moody, 1968.